How to Survive the Playground

A Handbook for Parents of Primary School Children

Sue Jones

chipmunkapublishing
the mental health publisher

Published by
Chipmunkapublishing
United Kingdom

http://www.chipmunkapublishing.com

ISBN   978-1-78382-140-2

Chipmunkapublishing gratefully acknowledge the support of Arts Council England.

When we think back to the playground at Primary school we may remember fun and games and friendships. We may also remember uncertainties and anxieties, and maybe even enemies.

What a rich experience our children will have......... and so will we as adults!

Parents often wait in the playground before and after school to drop off and collect their children. This special time can be a time to look forward to, or it can be a time to dread, or often somewhere in between. It is not just the children that have fun and games in the playground!

This book will tell you what your child (and you!) will experience in the exciting yet sometimes tension filled arena of the playground.

Sue Jones

This book is dedicated to

David and Katy

Sue Jones

About the Author

Sue Jones was born in Surrey and studied Psychology and Zoology at Reading University. She worked for many years at The Wellcome Foundation in Beckenham, before getting married and changing career direction. She is now an accredited counsellor who has been counselling for 20 years. She worked for Croydon Alcohol Counselling Service until its closure in 2010 and now works with Family Matters, a counselling organisation which is based in Gravesend. She lives with her husband and two children in West Wickham and it was here that she experienced both the joys and the anxieties of the school run. From these experiences this book was born!

Sue Jones

Acknowledgements

I would especially like to thank the following people for their input and enthusiasm about this book:

David, Katy, Sam and Grace for talking to me about the games they played in the playground and about the fun they had at break times.

Sally and Sarah for their input and interest in my earliest ideas.

Everyone who I met on the school run and the friendships I made along the way!

My husband, Steve, for helping me with computer issues and formatting some of the tables and diagrams.

My mother (now 95) for helping me with some spellings and grammar.

Ian for sharing his wisdom and thoughts about the shadow side of the playground.

And last but not least, Chipmunkapublishing for accepting this book, and for their kind and caring help and support during the publishing process.

Sue Jones

Contents

Sue Jones

Introduction

Very often when we think of school time we think of our children's education, their subjects, homework, exam results and sporting achievements. However there is one other area that is of great importance and I believe should be given greater attention. This other area is what children learn from playing in the playground.

In the playground children not only exercise and let off steam, they learn to cooperate with one another, they develop friendships and learn what works with others and what doesn't work. They make mistakes, they fall out with each other and they learn to make up. All this develops in complexity as children move through their Primary school years. Socialization, of course, has started at home, and been nurtured at preschool, but develops and grows through Primary school to become a building block and hopefully a firm foundation as children move from Primary school to Secondary school.

In addition, and what is little known about, is the unique experience parents can also have in the playground if they are regulars of the school run. School run mums and dads often wait inside the school playground at the beginning and end of the school day and what an experience that can be! This book is divided into two parts; the first part looking at the experience of the children in the playground and the second part describing the unique experience for parents.

The first part of this book, entitled **Children in the Playground**, aims to look at what happens to children in this arena and to look at some of the common experiences children have and what they can learn from them.

Chapter 1, The Playground – what does it offer?, looks at the playground as a space to use and describes what opportunities it offers to children. This chapter will include a pyramid diagram of opportunities which shows us the deeper levels of play.

Chapter 2, What Activities and Games go on in the Playground?, describes what children do in the playground. This looks at some of the games children play and the activities they get up to. It looks at how these games change over the years. Boys and girls often start out by playing together in a big group but as the years go by the sexes separate out. By the time the children are ready to start secondary school often the boys and girls have very separate activities.

So what do our children learn from their games and activities, apart from the enjoyment of these activities? **Chapter 3, What our Children Learn in the Playground**, looks at all the things that develop from playing. Children get an obvious enjoyment out of playing. It is fun and often good exercise. It is usually child initiated and gives children an element of control. Children learn to get along with one another and also develop friendships. They begin to learn what they like about one another and what things they find annoying! It is inevitable that children do fall out with one another and usually make up. Maybe they learn to say sorry.

Children can't get it right all the time, and sometimes they are not kind to one another, but overall they learn to get along. The building blocks of maturing socialization are firming up!

However this is not all that goes on in the playground – there is something else very interesting that goes on in this arena. Parents who take and collect their children from school spend some time in or near the playground. Parents may not be aware of it, but they experience something unique too. The second part of the book is called **Parents in the Playground.**

Chapter 4, Our Baby Starts 'Big' School, looks at the very first meetings for children and parents alike. It looks at our similarities and our differences and what different kinds of people we are likely to meet. It is likely to be one of the biggest variety of people we will meet anywhere. Both a joy and a challenge!

Chapter 5, The School Run, takes a light hearted look at this relentless daily activity of many parents. This chapter includes many examples from mums about the good things and the difficult things that they have experienced from taking their children to and from school and about spending some of that all important time standing and waiting in or just outside that playground.

Three big areas emerge for parents and I have devoted a chapter to each of these.

Chapter 6, Friendship and Support in the Playground, looks at the very positive aspect of the school run - being able to mix with a variety of different people and so find companionship and friendship. The closest friendships are often made with the parents of your child's good friends. These friendships are often special as we often share anxieties and worries about our children. We may go out for coffee, or see people in the evening and our social life will probably expand.

Another big area that seemed to come up as an issue for many mothers was one of comparison and anxiety -

a feeling of not being quite good enough when compared to others. **Chapter 7, Paranoia in the Playground**, looks at this issue. There is nothing new here as many mothers will ask themselves if they are being a good enough mother. However, if I am having a day of these sorts of doubts, there is nothing like standing in the playground for fuelling my anxieties! There is always someone there neater and tidier, there is always the mum who has managed to tidy her house and do all her ironing in one day, and the mum who has cooked the most wholesome tea for her children!

Chapter 8, Mother Tiger, Baby Cub (what affects you, affects me!), looks at the phenomenon of affect. In the chapter on Friendship and Support we look at how our special friends are often the mothers of our children's friends. However the very specialness of this friendship can be tarnished and damaged if our children fall out. Let us not kid ourselves that we are grown-up enough to rise above all this! We hurt for our children and feel sad and sometimes cross if their friendships falter. This is a unique parallel process that affects mother and child and their other relationships. It is the reason why friendships from the playground are so close, and yet because of the nature of the parent-child relationship the friendships are not independent like they would be at work, of if we were at college. This chapter looks at several situations that are unique to the playground.

The last chapter, **Chapter 9, Beginnings, Endings and Learning for all**, brings together a lot of what we have talked about and touched on in this book. It summarises how we all start out, as our children begin at Primary school, with our hopes and our fears, and how we all manage the transition through the years one way or another. This chapter looks at how the schools manage endings and how we, as parents, manage endings too and why it is sometimes more difficult for us to manage the transition. Never let it be said that parents do not gain anything, or learn something unique and exciting, from what is just the school run.

The playground looks from the outside as just a place where children run around and let off steam in their break time and lunchtime, but this book shows that it provides much more than that. **The playground is a unique space for children to learn how to be with one another – it provides the opportunity for children to develop advanced social skills.** The playground provides parents with special opportunities for friendship and learning too. Negotiating the anxiety, the friendships, the feuds and the fun brings all of us to a stronger place to start the next phase of our children's lives which will be the start of Secondary school.

Sue Jones

Part One

Children in the Playground

Sue Jones

Chapter 1
The Playground – what does it offer?

Thinking about the playground at Primary school conjures up memories of fun and games and friendship. We may also remember uncertainties and maybe even enemies. What a rich experience our children will have!

So what does the playground offer? Is it just a place to run around and let off steam in break time? Or does the playground offer much more? Looking at the obvious and not so obvious differences between being in class and being in the playground will help us start to find out about the exciting, yet sometimes tension filled, arena of the playground.

What is the playground?

The playground is intended as a safe space for children to play and it is a space that is not dominated by the teachers' influence. It is therefore an exciting and 'much looked forward to' time, but it can also be a daunting and scary place for younger children when they first start school.

Why do schools have a playground?

Young children are not able to sit still and concentrate for long periods of time and so it is important the school day is broken up into periods. In between the working periods the children go out to play if the weather is fine. If the weather is too wet then the breaks are taken inside. Often inside breaks are more structured than outside play as teachers will have to make sure that children are not running around the classrooms without any thought for the school property.

What are the main differences between being in class and being in the playground?

The differences may seem obvious and yet these are important as they enable our children to learn different (but no less important) things in each of these different areas.

In the classroom

When the children are in class their activities are usually taken at desks or in a group often sitting in front of the teacher (this is often a way of teaching for the younger years). The reason why teaching is done in this way is that the classroom size is limited and in order that all children can hear the teacher they need to be contained and their attention needs to be directed to the one person who is speaking and organising the activities. In the classroom then, the children's activities are controlled by the teacher and teaching assistants. The teacher always initiates the activities and directs proceedings. However if there are any difficulties with the activities there is always a teacher or teaching assistant present to help. In addition if there are any difficulties between children there is always someone adult to play referee.

In the playground

The most obvious difference from the classroom that the playground has to offer is much more space. The children are not contained in classrooms but are let free all together in a relatively unconfined space.

The second important difference is that the children are in contact with other classes. Sometimes all years play together in one large playground but often there are separate areas for different school years. For example the infant years (usually known as Reception, Year 1 and Year 2) may have an area all to themselves and the juniors (Years 3 and 4) may play together and in upper school (Years 5 and 6) the children may have their own well-defined space.

There are good reasons to separate the children in the playground, not least of all is the size of the children. From Reception to Year 6 the size difference is great and it is easy for younger children to get knocked over by older children.

Another good reason for keeping the years different is that the children have very different activities as they move though the school years and the playgrounds may have play equipment that is dedicated to the group of children who play there. For example, in the infant years, there may be some safe climbing equipment or toys that children may enjoy playing with. By the time children reach their upper school years more specific sports games may be played. It is not uncommon for serious games of football to be played in most break times. Games of tennis and cricket may also be played. Upper school playgrounds are likely to offer footballs and other sporting equipment. Often older children may have a hand in preparing and setting out the sporting equipment for playtime.

The next chapter, **Chapter 2, What Activities and Games go on in the Playground?**, provides a lot more detail on what children get up to.

The playground, therefore, offers more space and more freedom to move around and contact with other classes. It also offers the children more chance to interact socially than in the classroom and the freedom of choice regarding what they want to do.

Another very important thing - there is no teacher telling our children what to do! That is not to say that there are no adults present in the playground as there are always playground assistants who are present to monitor the overall activity in the playground and to help if someone falls and hurts themselves. These adults are sometimes teachers or teaching assistants but sometimes there are people who are employed especially for the purpose of helping at break time.

In the playground, however, there is no adult involved in the choice and spontaneity of the activities.

The children therefore choose:

- Who they want to play with
- What they want to do, and
- How long that activity is going to last.

These choices are sometimes fraught with difficulty, but as you can see by **Chapter 3, What our Children Learn in the Playground**, these first negotiations are the very building blocks of all that goes on in our adult life. Negotiations, good and bad, take place hour by hour in all the great organisations of our working life. Negotiations, good and bad, are fundamental to all our relationships and learning to negotiate well is a very great skill indeed. Never let it be said that children are 'just' playing.

Of course there are other social skills besides negotiating and the playground offers children more chance for spontaneous social interactions than in the classroom. Friendships will develop from play and the children will begin to develop the all important skill of empathy, learning to understand how other people feel. These skills do not develop overnight and often mistakes have to be made in order for children to learn that they have upset someone. Therefore the playground also has the potential for more upset and difficulty than in the classroom. In the classroom difficulties can be controlled and nipped in the bud to a large degree, but in the playground things can go unnoticed. Realistically there is the potential for struggles and difficulties in the playground.

The differences between the classroom and the playground can be summarised as follows:

In the classroom:

- There is a space limitation and the activities are mainly sedentary
- The activities are structured
- The interactions between children are controlled by the teacher and teaching assistant
- Help is provided when there are difficulties with the activity or if there is difficulty with interactions between children.

In the playground:

- More space
- More freedom
- Contact with other classes
- Freedom of choice
- More spontaneous activities
- Limited control of activities by adults

- More social interactions
- More potential for difficulties

What does the playground offer our little ones?

I expect there are lots of mothers who, in the early days, have passed by their children's playground and had a little look. These mums look to see if they can see their child playing, to make sure they are happy and maybe to make sure they are not all by themselves. I know I have!

So what do we notice about playgrounds if we are close by. I guess the first thing that we would notice is the noise – happy children playing make a lot of noise! Another thing that we would notice if we were able to peep through the hedge would be the activity. The whole playground will seem at first to be a mass of children running around in all directions. One thing it seems to offer is exercise and fresh air and a place to let off steam. At first there seems to be little structure to this mass of activity, but any teacher on playground duty will tell you that there is much structure to the playtime. The children form into groups big and small and begin playing games. The excitement can be huge. The playground offers fun and games for our children and we hope that through this playing our children will begin to form friendships.

Children begin to learn social skills from birth as we smile and interact with our new baby. These skills are developed and nurtured as babies become toddlers and then begin preschool. It is here at preschool that many children have a first experience of being with many children of their own age. Children arrive at Primary school with basic social skills and these develop as children go through Primary school. Time in the playground allows children to develop social skills in a more spontaneous way than at preschool where it is expected that children's interactions are monitored more closely.

By the time children have reached Year 6 they are already developing quite advanced social skills such as empathy and negotiation. In addition, most children will have had some difficult times in class or in the playground (and as parents we hope not too difficult!). However the children are learning how to deal with difficult situations. So, in a roundabout way, some difficulty can only be strengthening and will help children negotiate life's more difficult times.

In summary the playground offers a multitude of positive things including:

- Fresh air
- Time to exercise and let off steam
- Fun and games
- Friendship
- Basic social skills
- More advanced social skills such as negotiation and empathy
- Dealing with difficult situations

Diagram 1, A pyramid diagram of opportunities, may help us to remember these very important things in a more pictorial way. The bottom part of the diagram (our foundation) shows us the obvious opportunities playtime provides for our children, while towards the apex of the pyramid are the learning opportunities that we may not think of at first. These are the more advanced social skills that are developing all the way through Primary school years and all the way through life as it turns out.

Diagram 1

A pyramid diagram of opportunities that playtime offers our children

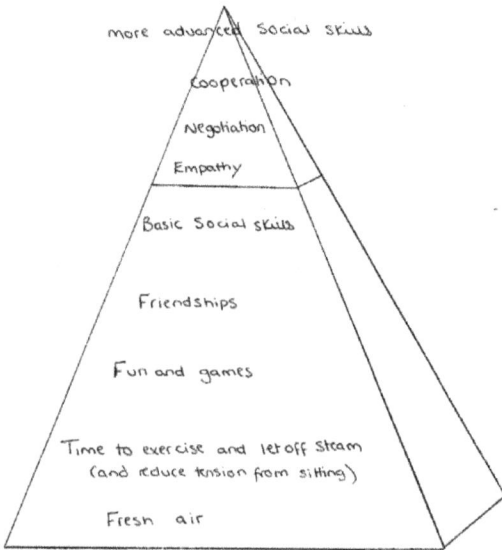

more advanced Social skills

Cooperation

Negotiation

Empathy

Basic Social skills

Friendships

Fun and games

Time to exercise and let off steam (and reduce tension from sitting)

Fresh air

Looking a little deeper at the opportunities playtime provides for our children will help us to value this time and begin to realise what a rich and vital part of development stems from this time.

Chapter 2
What Activities and Games go on in the Playground?

When children of different ages were asked **'What is the best thing about playing in the playground?'** their answers leave us in no doubt about the enjoyment of playtime. Some of the answers are documented below:

The best things about playing in the playground

"Playing games like football and basketball"

"Playing with my friends"

"The apparatus"

"Chase games"

"Football"

"No work!"

"Cricket and pat ball"

"Talking to my friends"

"Playing mummies and daddies"

"Playing with my football cards"

"Cricket and grab ball"

"Running about"

"Playing Spiderman!"

It is clear from these answers that the children enjoy a variety of games and activities, some of which are structured activities like football and cricket, some are imaginary activities like playing mummies and daddies and Spiderman. My son particularly enjoyed playing Dr Who. The activities that children prefer generally depend on their age and sex and in the next section we will look at this in more detail.

In this chapter I have chosen to look at what goes on in the playground under three different headings:

- Different games and activities

- What children talk about

- What difficult things happen in the playground

Different Games and Activities

There are a huge number of different games that are played in the playground and a few of these have been mentioned above. The activities usually change depending on age and the complexity of some of these activities change over time.

Infant play

Young children often (but not always) play in larger groups. They often play games where everyone can play together. Games that are very popular are Chase, and Circle games like Duck Duck Goose. Rhyming games and skipping games are also enjoyed in large or small groups. Boys and girls play happily together and often really enjoy each other's company. The first few years at school are often happy, uncomplicated times. Of course there is a reason for this – the children don't know each other very well when they start school and so although they may be able to say whether they like someone or not, or whether someone is naughty or not, their social skills and ability to play complex games is limited. Uncomplicated all-inclusive games are often the norm.

Middle school

Children begin to develop firm friendships in their infant years and these are further strengthened in the middle school years. By now children know who they like and who they don't like and are less likely to play in big groups. By now it is clear that the boys and girls are often enjoying games that are more specific to their own gender. Girls enjoy playing animal games or games from TV or musicals and boys are busy playing football and playing with cards and various collections depending on the craze at the time e.g. football cards. Chase games are still popular with boys and girls and these include 'It' and 'Stuck in the Mud'. As the groups children play in get smaller and more specific, there is more room for difficulties! This will be discussed later in this chapter.

Upper school

In the upper school years the children are beginning to show a sign of maturity and with that a more sophisticated approach to games and social interactions. Boys and girls often play entirely separately and it is not uncommon by Year 6 for some of the girls to be showing some sort of interest in boys in the realms of boyfriends and girlfriends. Games that are played are often more structured and boys and girls often play a sport at lunchtime. In many schools the playgrounds are set up with sporting equipment in order to encourage games that may have been taught in sports lessons. Often children are given the responsibility for setting out equipment that might be used during playtime.

Whatever the differences between the years with regard to games and activities, the enthusiasm for a break from lessons goes undiminished!

Table 1, Playtime activities in Primary school years, summarises the activities mentioned above and distinguishes between boys and girls activities where they may be different. It is important to remember that this table only gives a brief summary of some of the popular games and activities in Great Britain. I am sure a whole book could be written on all the types of games and activities played around the world.

What children talk about

This is obviously a big subject and I can only scratch the surface, but I have tried to give an overview on this fascinating area.

Children of all years will talk in various degrees of complexity and understanding about most of the following topics:

- Things going on at home

- Things going on in school including the teachers

- Things about other children in their class

- Who has what

- Who is doing what

- Who is going out with who

- Important topics, like sex

Things going on at home

Children will talk about what goes on at home even if it makes parents cringe! However it is not just the difficult things that children will discuss; children will talk about the exciting things too e.g. the arrival of a new pet or a sibling's birthday. Sometimes talking about sad things with a friend will really help when something very sad has happened like the death of a much loved grandparent.

Things going on in school including the teachers

Often exciting things are going on in school and these events will be talked about in the playground e.g. a visiting theatre or the visit of a sporting celebrity. Children talk about what is going on in their lessons, probably not so much the content of the lesson but what might have happened if someone has been naughty. Children will talk kindly of the teachers that they like and less kindly of the teachers who they don't like. They will talk about being told off themselves especially if they feel that the telling off was unfair. Talking about teachers who are a bit frightening may help to lessen the anxiety especially if several children all feel the same.

Things about other children in their school

As much as we would like to think that our child doesn't say anything too unkind about another child it is likely that most children will talk about other children they like and about those they dislike. No different from us then! We hope that when they do talk about other children in the school it is not within earshot of the other child if what they are saying is not kind.

Who has what?

This is the annoying one! There are always children in school who seem to have more of everything and so make our children discontent. In fact these children often enjoy sharing their good fortune which is not always a blessing. However it is one of the hard lessons in life - some people have more than you, and some people have less.

Who is doing what?

Children are very astute when it comes to keeping an eye on what other children are getting up to. Who has borrowed my rubber and forgotten to give it back, right up to who was cheating on their times table test. Also children are very aware of who is being kind and who is being unkind. Conversations may centre on who said something unkind to someone and made them cry, for example.

Who is going out with whom?

This topic is much discussed by girls as they reach the end of their Primary school years. Obviously the 'going out' is not usually what we mean by 'going out' as adults, although there may be some exceptions.

Mainly it is a loose term for being paired with someone in school. The active, sporty, handsome boys are often quite sought after!

Important topics

Important topics like sex are discussed. It is not uncommon for younger children to come home and tell us who said what about how babies are made. This could be the time for sex education at home. Death and dying are discussed too, especially if this is relevant to losing a loved one at home. Different faiths are discussed and so are important festivals that are celebrated. Other topics such as football and other sporting events are important topics especially for the boys.

In a nutshell, children talk about all the things that grown-ups talk about! They strengthen connections with each other by talking, and reduce anxieties by talking about their difficult situations. Some of the talk is fun, and some of it is not, but having the opportunity to talk and socialise is a vital part of our wellbeing. The time in the playground offers our children this opportunity.

What difficult things happen in the playground?

Let's now look at the shadow side of the playground. I asked several children another question. **'What difficult things have happened to you in the playground?'**

Here are some of their answers:

"Not being chosen to play"

"My best friend going off with another friend"

"Being left out"

"Having a big argument with my friend"

"Having disagreements during a football game about rules"

"Someone taking over a game"

"Half way through a nice game someone suddenly doesn't want to play anymore"

"Someone taking a part in a game that you were meant to be doing"

"When everyone talks over you"

"The team being cross when I didn't score"

"Falling over and badly hurting my knee"

I guess these are all fairly common occurrences in the playground and most children will experience at least some of these happening to them. These occurrences are upsetting and can ruin a playtime but it is probably 'part and parcel' of being at school. I expect we can all remember some of the same upsetting experiences from our own school days. In **Chapter 3, What our Children Learn in the Playground**, I discuss whether some of these events can help our children grow stronger as they learn to weather the knocks of life. The occurrences mentioned above are not considered to be bullying unless the event is consistently repeated towards one child over a period of time.

Bullying

While some of the above occurrences could turn into bullying if they are repeated over time (e.g. being consistently left out of games) most of the occurrences mentioned above are usually one-off, on the spur of the moment, events. **Bullying is altogether different from the occasional upsetting event and is a repeated activity directed at one child over time**. Bullying is an activity that is aimed at upsetting a particular child and is a repeated activity over days, weeks and sometimes even months and years. Most schools have policies in place to stop bullying and everything should be done to prevent this damaging activity. The next chapter looks at bullying in more detail.

Shouting, Fighting and Verbal Abuse

To some extent this will go on at all schools. There will always be boys who will shout and get in a fight with another and there will always be girls who will shout hateful things at each other. It is not always enemies that get into this situation, sometimes it is children who are quite close or who are attracted to each other in some way, that end up having fights and big arguments. Often these children end up friends again after the argument. However it is important that children don't hurt each other during a fight and it is important that playground helpers are vigilant to these heated arguments that can flare up quite quickly. Also some children do use bad language and this should be nipped in the bud as not all children know all the bad words used in our society. Sad to say that they will probably know them all by the time they leave Primary school!

Summary

This chapter has looked at some of the things that go on in the playground. It has covered the following topics:

- The best things about playing in the playground

- The games and activities of the playground

- What children talk about in the playground

- The difficult things that happen in the playground (including fighting, shouting and bullying)

We are beginning to see just how important the playground is and what special things go on there. There is the obvious enjoyment of all the games and activities but it is also the place where children learn to talk and share, and deepen friendships. They learn that sharing an anxiety can be helpful, talking about the death of a loved one can help with sadness, and that talking about happy things can make them feel good.

However in the playground there are more opportunities for intense emotions, which may lead to the difficult things that can occur there too. In the next chapter we will discuss whether some difficulties can strengthen children for their life ahead.

Table 1
Playtime activities in the Primary school years

Years	Boys	Girls
Infants (Years R, 1 & 2)	Football (when balls are allowed) Large group games eg Duck Duck Goose Rhyming games Chase games Animal games Home games	Skipping games Large group games eg Duck Duck Goose Rhyming games Chase games Animal games Home games
Middle school (Years 3 and 4)	Sports eg football Looking at cards/collections Latest craze! Playing games from TV or films eg Dr Who or Spiderman Chase games eg It, Stuck in the Mud	Animal games Playing games from TV, films or musicals Singing, Dancing Chase games eg It, Stuck in the Mud
Upper school (Years 5 and 6)	Sports eg football, cricket, tennis etc Playing with cards and collections Chase games (sometimes with girls!)	Sports eg football, netball, tennis, basket ball etc Chatting in groups Playing games or singing songs from musicals Dancing

Sue Jones

Chapter 3
What our Children Learn in the Playground

When I first started thinking about this chapter, I jotted down a mind map of all the things I could think of that are learning points for children. These thoughts can be viewed in Diagram 2. All these varied topics made me realise that what we learn from the playground is vital for making our way in the world. I have grouped these topics under the following headings:

- Basic social skills
- Learning how to be a friend
- Learning how to get along in a group
- Dealing with difficult situations and emotions
- Advanced social skills
- What is 'not OK' behaviour
- Important lessons in life

Obviously these skills don't just develop from playing in the playground. Learning begins at home. Learning carries on before and after school, at weekends and in the holidays. However the playground is unique, as we have seen in Chapters 1 and 2, and provides our children with an environment that cannot be provided elsewhere.

Basic Social Skills

Basic social skills (talking, listening and the art of conversation) begin at home and our children will bring to the playground their own unique way of interacting with others. Some children are naturally chatty and outgoing and others are quieter. Some are bursting with energy, some are more anxious, while some are quiet and calm. Many of these traits are genetic – the unique blueprint of our children. However, on top of this, are the experiences of our environment. Are we encouraged to be talkative? Do we have someone who will listen to us and understand what we are saying? Is our energy encouraged and delighted in? Or are we encouraged to be quiet and good? All these things will influence how we develop our basic social skills as children.

From this starting point, children arrive at school with their own amazing uniqueness and the variety is never-ending! At preschool and at 'big' school children begin immediately to practise and develop their social skills.

So what do we mean by basic social skills? These are the skills children have already started to acquire at home and which develop throughout the school years. They include:

- Listening
- Talking
- Interacting
- The art of conversation

Listening

Talking and listening go hand in hand with any conversation, but listening is not as easy as it first seems. We may not be talking when someone else is talking, but are we really hearing what the other person is saying? This is a skill that we can all do with practising all through life. At school children are taught to listen in class. No wonder children want to talk when they get 'out to play'.

Talking

Some children like to talk all the time; they are often sunny and cheerful children. But without learning to listen and hear what the other is saying, there is no real conversation. Often a talkative child will find a quieter child to talk to, but more often than not, talkative children are attracted to each other, and quieter children find more space and companionship with a quieter child.

Interacting

Interacting brings together talking and listening. When children are little this may be fairly simple. The children often talk about what is happening in their lives but they may not respond directly to what another child is saying as can be seen in the simple conversation below:

Jenny: 'I'm getting a kitten for my birthday!'
Jack: 'My Auntie's got a dog and I take him for walks'

This is an interaction and the response of Jack is linked by the topic of an animal but not relating directly to the comment by Jenny.

The art of conversation

This is more complex than the example given above. Jack now responds to Jenny's comment in a way that is directly related to what she is saying.

Jenny: 'I'm getting a kitten for my birthday!'
Jack: 'Lucky you, what will you call it?'

Learning how to be a friend

What an important skill to learn!

Thinking of any friend that we may have – what qualities do we want in them? My list is as follows:

- Someone to listen to me
- Someone to have fun with
- Someone who is loyal and doesn't talk about me behind my back
- Someone who doesn't go off with someone else when they get bored, or if things get difficult
- Someone who likes me and is on my side
- Someone who doesn't judge me
- Someone who has common interests

Hang on! This is all very well for adults, but for someone who is only five, this is a very tall order. Or is it? Looking back at Chapter 2, some of the upsetting incidents in the playground related to friends going off with other people, and friends leaving you out etc. It is clear then, that friendship will involve some or all of the above qualities to a certain degree. Children learn as they go along about friendship and what is important to them. Not all children are the same. Some children put more of an importance on loyalty, whereas others will seek out fun and excitement. Boys will often seek out someone they can share an activity with (e.g. football) and so common interests are important in this situation.

Learning how to get along in a group

Getting along in a group is very important if we want to work in organisations as adults, or even if we want to belong to an activity group. Getting on in a group is important to us socially, and there is no better learning experience than being in the playground. After all we may not like everyone in our group, but sometimes we need to learn to get along with individuals for the benefit of the group. Of course most of us have been in a group from the moment we have been born (our family group) so this social skill has been developing from the very beginning.

So what makes a group?

It is the things that join us together:

- Common interest
- Common activities
- Shared vision
- Friendship

Let's take two different but very common groups seen in the playground.

The football teams

The children who form these groups all have football as an interest to a greater or lesser degree. They all enjoy playing football and all want to develop and show off their skills. The team will have a shared vision of being the best! And finally the team will learn some rules - everyone needs to put the group before their own individuality. This is often a difficult lesson to learn.
What a lot of learning just from one game of football.

Singing and acting groups

Often groups of children will enjoy singing and acting from popular musicals. The children who make up these groups all enjoy musicals and choose a particular musical as a focus. High School Musical was popular when my children were at Primary school. They enjoy singing, dancing and acting and they share a vision of maybe performing in such a musical. Again there has to be some give and take as to what tunes are sung and what parts are acted - often a cause of some debate and negotiation!

Of course children learn how to be in groups in the classroom and often perform group activities in a more formal and structured manner. However as the next section shows, the playground, due to its unstructured nature, allows for more mistakes, more difficulties, but ultimately more learning of a social nature.

Dealing with difficult situations and emotions

Looking back at **Chapter 2, What Activities and Games go on in the Playground?** I asked children what difficult things happen in the playground. These difficulties can be summarised as follows:

- Being left out
- Rejection
- Disagreements and arguments
- Someone taking over a game or a situation
- Someone not playing by the rules
- Being ridiculed and admonished by the group
- Not being listened to by the group

Along with these difficult situations are the difficult emotions that can go with them:

- Sadness
- Envy
- Anger
- Irritation
- Frustration
- Feeling shame
- Feeling not heard

Table 2 links the difficult situations with possible emotions felt by children. How difficult it is for little children to go through these situations and feel these emotions. No wonder there are often tears and tantrums, and sometimes cross words, and even some pushing and hitting out in the playground.

Resolving difficult situations

If there has been a difficult situation, and some difficult feelings experienced, the next step is expression of those feelings (or the holding on to those feelings). Let's take a couple of examples:

Being left out leads to **sadness and anxiety** which may lead to **crying** (expression of feeling).

Not unreasonably little children (and older ones!) may cry when they are left out. As children get older they may learn to hold on to their feelings and express them in a different way as the next example illustrates:

Being left out leads to **sadness and anxiety** which may lead to **deciding to find someone else to play with!**

Let's take another example:

Argument with friend leads to **anger, irritation and frustration** which may lead to **hitting out** or **crying**.

Little children may hit out in this situation or may cry, but as they grow more mature they learn (hopefully!) to express themselves in a way that may get a better response.

Argument with friend leads to **anger, irritation and frustration** which may lead to **discussing what is wrong and trying to negotiate or cooperate.**

Looking down the list of difficult situations, I expect we can all remember some, if not all, of these things happening to us at school. Nobody wants their children to have difficult situations but some are, I think, inevitable. Some of these situations can teach our children valuable lessons about dealing with powerful emotions.

Advanced social skills

As the children move through the years at Primary school, they will learn more advanced social skills.

These social skills include:

- Negotiation
- Cooperation
- Empathy
- Initiating play/leadership qualities

Negotiation

I have given a simple example of where negotiation would be helpful in the previous section on dealing with difficult situations and emotions. Often negotiation comes from trying to change a situation that does not meet our needs. In the previous example, where a child may feel anger, irritation and frustration towards a friend, instead of hitting out (or walking away and saying nothing) the child may try to negotiate so that the other person may see their point of view. This may help to change the situation.

Negotiation skills are also needed when children have strong minds about what they want to do!

Cooperation

Cooperating together means give and take. Cooperating is learning that sometimes doing things for the good of the group or for the good of your relationship makes for a more harmonious group or relationship. Some children (and adults) are naturally more cooperative than others.

Empathy

Empathy can be described as being able to stand in someone else's shoes and understand how they are feeling. Some people have high levels of empathy whereas others have less. It is believed that this ability to be empathic may be genetically predetermined and children on the Autistic Spectrum will find the skills of empathy and mentalization difficult. Mentalization is the ability to determine what people are thinking by understanding their mental state from their behaviour.

Initiating play/leadership qualities

This is about assertiveness and being proactive in putting forward ideas and thoughts about what to play. It is the beginning of leadership qualities and some children seem to be natural born leaders, while others are happier being a member of a team or group.

The four skills of negotiation, cooperation, empathy and leadership are big grown-up skills.

What's 'not-ok' behaviour
(the inevitable bad behaviours)

The number of times my children had come home from school and told me about something that had happened at school. This told me that they were learning about what was 'not-ok' behaviour. Here are some of their examples:

'This boy pushed someone right over!'

'Someone said the f-word, mummy! They said it really loudly!'

'So-and-so stole my rubber; I saw them put it in their desk!'

'This poor girl started crying because all her friends were so mean to her'

'They wouldn't let so-and-so play football. They said he wasn't good enough!'

Most children instantly know what constitutes bad behaviour:

- Pushing
- Hitting
- Shouting
- Swearing
- Stealing
- Being mean

All these behaviours will go on in every school and children will watch and observe. Often the line between right and wrong will be strengthened as they watch others. Sometimes boys can be physical and generally are more likely to push each other and shout at each other than girls, but this is a general rule and not always the case! Girls are sometimes mean to each other verbally, saying things that are unkind.

Children will learn what is right and wrong from the playground and often behaviours may slowly change as the children develop socially from infants to seniors. A child who is often outspoken and sometimes mean may learn that this doesn't always help to develop deep friendships. She may learn to contain her behaviour. A child, who may sometimes miss out on playtime because the playground helper has admonished them for pushing others about, may learn that it is better not to do this.

However, patterns of behaviour start at home and are sometimes difficult to change. A child who is often pushed around by older brothers may believe that this is acceptable behaviour and follow on doing this at school. Of course he may like to get his own back on smaller children if he is always pushed around by bigger individuals. Likewise, a girl who has several older sisters, who are a bit mean to her and leave her out of their activities, may develop similar traits as she plays at school.

Bullying

Bad behaviour that happens now and again is inevitable, but if one child is consistently targeted by another child or children over a period of time, then this is considered to be bullying. A child who is consistently left out or ignored by others can have a miserable and despairing life at school. It is no wonder, then, that most schools do have policies in place to help children who are being bullied. Sometimes there are mentoring schemes where younger children can talk to an older child and sometimes one of the teachers is a coordinator for help with bullying and will be an approachable adult in times of difficulty.

Table 3 shows of some examples of different types of bullying that can take place.

Bullying often seems to start with a difference. Children who are different from the norm are more likely to be noticed, and more likely to be the target of attention. However the victim of the bully has to be upset by the teasing or resulting behaviour in order for the bullying to be effective. For example, someone who isn't bothered whether they are good at games or not, may just laugh off any teasing or name calling. Bullies need a victim that cares and is upset about the behaviour of the bully; in this way the victim and bully become a unit and cannot exist without each other.

There are many books that have been written on bullying, and some of these have been referenced for further exploration of this important topic.

Important lessons in life

Finally, and no less important than all the other aspects that have been mentioned, children learn important lessons in life as they mature through Primary school. Their time spent 'playing' in the playground can contribute greatly to these very important lessons.

Learning to rub along with people we don't like

We may not like everybody but we may need to get along with others. It would be easier if we liked everybody we had to be with, but the reality is that there will be some people who we have to rub shoulders with who we don't like.

Learning to say 'sorry', forgiving and making up

Oh so important at all ages! And not so easy either! It helps us in life if we start learning this important lesson at home and in the playground.

Learning to stand up for yourself

Another very important lesson. To feel confident and to be able to stand up for ourselves if others think differently to us, and not to lose touch with our own sense of self, is such a help to us all as we go through life.

Recognising and celebrating differences

School time will bring a wide variety of children together. This can cause difficulties but on the whole children are very open to different ideas and new views. From my own experience children are often fascinated by differences in religion and culture, but less comfortable with a family who has a higher disposable income. Children (and adults!) will make comparisons with others and feel envy and jealously. Learning that we have more than some people but less than others, and learning that people are different in some ways but are essentially the same in many areas, is an important lesson in life.

Learning who we like, and who we don't like, and why

This can sometimes take children a long time to learn while some children seem to know quickly and astutely who they like and who they don't like. Sometimes children are attracted to the chattiest and most pretty girl or the boy who is best at football, but only time will tell if these qualities are also associated with good friendship skills. Sometimes children who are very accommodating will make friends with a child who likes their own way. This child may not always treat their friend well. So often, we as parents, hear of children who are nice to our children one day, and then have a different friend the next day. If our child is very accommodating they will forgive the other child and be glad to have their friendship back when it suits the other child. Sometimes it takes a long time for children to realise what makes a good friend.

Learning about competitiveness

Being competitive is important in the world, as in the long run it will help us compete for jobs and become successful in the world. School life is competitive to a degree, and competition is encouraged in sporting activities and some activities in the classroom. Sporting activities can be structured as in game lessons or more spontaneous, such as games initiated in the playground. Some competitiveness should be encouraged but not at the expense of everything else!

Summary of Chapter 3, What Children Learn in the Playground

This chapter aims to illustrate how important 'just playing' really is! Our children are not just running around and letting off steam after being cooped up in class. Of course getting fresh air and exercise is an important part of playtime but it is not the only thing that is going on. The important building blocks of mature socialization are developing too. This is such an important part of our lives that we should pay more attention to this aspect of school life.

This chapter has covered the following important topics:

- Basic social skills
- Learning how to be a friend
- Learning how to get along in a group
- Dealing with difficult situations and emotions
- Advanced social skills
- What is 'not OK' behaviour
- Important lessons in life

Table 4 summarises all that we have looked at in this chapter.

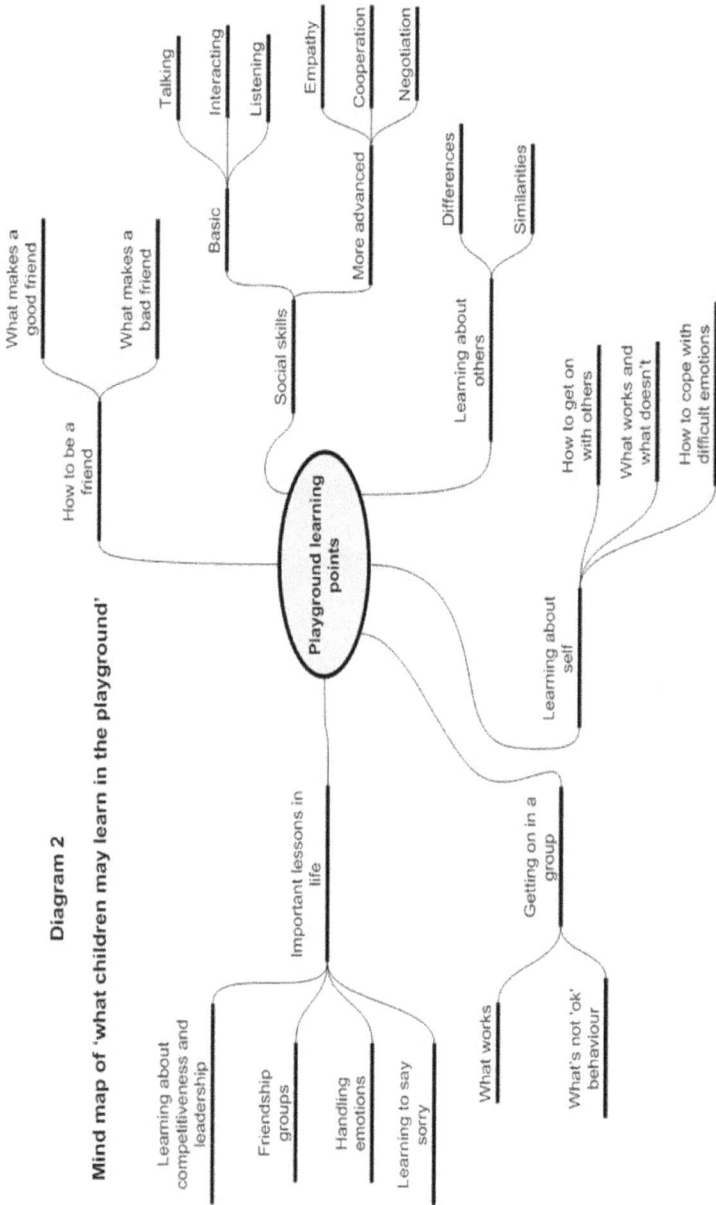

Diagram 2

Mind map of 'what children may learn in the playground'

- **Playground learning points**

  - How to be a friend
    - What makes a good friend
    - What makes a bad friend

  - Social skills
    - Basic
      - Talking
      - Interacting
      - Listening
    - More advanced
      - Empathy
      - Cooperation
      - Negotiation

  - Learning about others
    - Differences
    - Similarities

  - Learning about self
    - How to get on with others
    - What works and what doesn't
    - How to cope with difficult emotions

  - Important lessons in life
    - Learning about competitiveness and leadership
    - Friendship groups
    - Handling emotions
    - Learning to say sorry

  - Getting on in a group
    - What works
    - What's not 'ok' behaviour

Table 2
Difficult situations and possible emotions felt by children

Difficult situation	Possible feelings and emotions
Being left out	Sadness Anxiety Envy
Rejection	Sadness Anger Jealousy
Disagreements and arguments	Anger Irritation Frustration
'Bossy boots' taking over a situation (eg a game)	Anger Frustration
Someone not playing by the rules	Anger Frustration
Being ridiculed and admonished by the group (eg team being cross at bad play)	Sadness Anger Shame
Not being listened to by the group	Anxiety Anger at not being heard

Table 3
Types of bullying situations

Situation	Possible reasons for bullying
Children who are different to look at	Noticing what somebody wears or their shape
Different cultures or religions	Fear of difference
Children who are not good at games	Amusement out of someone's failure
Children who are especially gifted	Children may be seen as too much of a 'Clever Clogs'
Children who have different accents	Amusement at copying another's accent
Children with behaviour problems	Enjoyment out of causing pain to another with difficulty
Children with learning difficulties	Enjoyment/amusement of picking on the weakest

Table 4
Summary of what children learn in the playground

Learning points	Skills and knowledge
Basic social skills	Listening Talking Interacting The art of conversation
Learning how to be a friend	Qualities of 'good' friendship Different people like different qualities
Learning how to get on in a group	What brings groups of people together
Dealing with difficult situations and emotions	How to handle people Becoming more robust
Advanced social skills	Negotiation Cooperation Empathy Initiating play/leadership qualities
What's 'not-ok' behaviour	Differences between types of behaviour
Important lessons in life	Getting along with all! Learning to say 'sorry' Learning to stand up for yourself Recognising and celebrating difference Learning who we get on with The importance of competitiveness

Sue Jones

Part 2

Parents in the Playground

Sue Jones

Chapter 4
Our Baby Starts 'Big' School
(Meeting the other children and parents for the first time)

It may seem logical to think that the first time that we meet the other parents and children will be on the very first day, but usually the school will have had an introductory morning or afternoon before the first day.

Introductory morning or afternoon

A very common scenario is that the parents and children come to the new school on a prearranged date. After a little talk or presentation by the school form teacher or the head teacher, the children may be gathered together by their new form teacher, perhaps for a story, and the parents will be left to chat over a cup of tea or coffee. The initial meeting with the new teacher may only be an hour or so, but this will give us all our first impressions. And usually at first they are good ones. Everyone (teachers, parents and children) are trying their very best to be good and friendly! The teacher seems good and kind, the other children seem sweet and friendly (some may even be a little overawed and there may be a few tears) and the other mothers, even if they don't all immediately seem the same as us, do at least seem friendly and wanting to talk. Everyone wants their child to be happy at school and it is a big step moving on from preschool to 'big' school. Most of us are a little anxious and I think this makes the adults more friendly and ready to share their experiences. If we are lucky we may already know some of the children and mums from 'our' preschool days and if the children have at least one or two friends in their class then we will feel more comfortable about the start of 'big' school.

The first day

The build up to the first day can be quite stressful especially if it is your first child going to 'big' school. All the things that need to be done seem never-ending: making sure you have the correct uniform in the correct size, making sure you have the school bag, lunch box, and that all the forms are correctly filled in. When the practical side is complete there is still the mental preparation for your child and even more importantly for yourself! This is the end of babyhood and while there is celebration and excitement for your child about moving on, for a mother it also constitutes an ending with feelings of loss. Our baby is no longer so dependent on us and is about to begin the path to adulthood and maturity.

Your child is likely to be quite excited about starting 'big' school and encouragement and enthusiasm from parents can go a long way to helping children start on their first day with much anticipation and few anxieties. However let's not forget that starting Primary school can also be a big step for us mums, especially if it is our first child. We will probably have far more anxieties than our child as the following questions illustrate:

- Will they be happy?
- Will they make friends?
- Will the other children be nice?
- Will he sit next to a good child or a naughty one?
- Will he be bullied?
- Will he remember to go to the toilet?
- Will the teacher like him?
- Will he like his teacher?

- Will he like his lunch?
- Will he miss his mummy?

While it is inevitable that we may feel stressed by all that is going on - things to organise, anxiety about the first day and the process of starting to let go, it is important not to worry too much in front of our child. Anxious mummies can make anxious children. Anxieties are natural but being upbeat about the new start is important, as well as talking to your child about any anxieties they may have. As a rule, we as parents, should share our own anxieties with each other or other mums and not with our children as many of our anxieties will come to nothing. Most children settle into school well without anything untoward happening, and parents have a key role in helping their child start school with a sense of excitement and enthusiasm.

But here we are on the first day, the start of the school run years for many mums and some dads. It is now time to start preparing for our own survival in the playground!

Mostly everyone is friendly at first

The very beginning of my children's start at school was actually one of the best times for me. Mostly everyone is trying to be friendly and it can feel very nice and fun to suddenly know a big group of people which you feel part of. Often the mums may go out for a meal or to the pub for an evening, in order to facilitate friendships and to talk about the school and how the children are settling in. In my son's class many of the mums and dads would meet in the park next to the school. It soon became a regular after school activity to go to the park with biscuits and drinks so that the adults could talk and the children could play together.

First Impressions

However friendly people are, there are of course differences, and people do have different values. Some differences are obvious right from the start, and these are to do with what we can see and hear, these are our first impressions. Differences between people are interesting and exciting and they shouldn't necessarily cause problems. Some differences (like values) take time to discover and sometimes can cause difficulties if we have different values about parenting.

Obvious differences

At first, when we meet people, the obvious differences come from what we can see and hear:

- What do they look like? Do they seem friendly?
- What do they like talking about?

These will be the first thing that we will notice on first meeting someone. No wonder we make a bit of an effort here!

What do we look like?

What we look like will include:

- Age
- Clothes
- Appearance

Here are some examples of what some mums have to say on this tricky topic:

'I have sometimes felt anxious about this because I have not fallen into the young, smart, 'a different outfit everyday' type of mummy. I don't fit the so called 'Yummy Mummy' label and feel a bit in awe of those who do!'

'I was pleased to see that a lot of the mums made an effort with what they looked like – it made me feel as if they were like me and cared about their appearance'

'I was the oldest mother in my daughter's class and have never really been that interested in what I wear on a day to day basis. There were also a lot of very young mothers who looked great so that probably made me feel a little different! Mind you, if I had been 35 and not in my 50s I would probably have been just as glamorous!'

Whether we like to admit it or not, we all sum up other people by what we see and hear. When my son first started school I did indeed make more of an effort for the school run. I always used to wear my lipstick! Everyone is aware of everyone else at some level, although maybe not consciously. The process of observing others is at work whether we are aware of it or not.

What do we like talking about?

We are often attracted to people who like talking about similar things but the variety of conversations between parents can be huge. I have listed some of the topics that can be heard in the playground:

- What's happening in the school
- How our children are getting on
- Problems with our children
- How well our children are doing
- What we are doing at the week-end
- The weather
- Ironing
- Shopping (food/clothes)
- What we are wearing, and complimenting others
- What we are doing today
- What other people are wearing
- What other mothers have done
- What other children have done
- What other mothers have said
- What other children have said
- Who is going to who's party
- What is happening in the news

Well of course the list is endless and people talk about almost everything. I was amused and impressed that mothers do talk with genuine passion about how much ironing they had to do – they would talk about it at drop off and tell you how many hours they had done at pick up! I expect they have nice tidy houses too and maybe you are beginning to guess that mine is not so tidy....

However, conversation is the beginning of friendships and it is through conversation that we will begin to see if people have similar values to us. We don't have to be best friends with everyone, but to deepen the relationship to friendship, we must like what we see, be interested in what we hear and share some life values.

Our life values

Our life values include those things that we believe in and those beliefs guide us in how we conduct our life. Some values that you may hold as a mother may include the following:

- My children should be clean and neat most of the time
- My children should be allowed a lot of freedom
- Homework should always be done and handed in on the right day
- Children should not have to worry about getting dirty if they play outdoors
- What does it matter if my children get nits?
- Children's education should come as a first priority
- Children's time should always be filled with activities

This list, like so many others, can go on and on, but even looking at this short list we can see that there are some values that we agree with and some that we don't. It is difficult being really good friends with someone whose values are very different. Here are some examples:

'I like my children to look tidy and I felt cross when my daughter went to a birthday tea dressed in her party outfit and come back covered in mud because the children had all been playing in the garden in March!'

'I worry about my children catching nits and I am quite obsessive about using a nit comb once a week. I was shocked when I found out that a child had come to school and the mother knew she had nits!

'It seems such a shame for that little boy – he is never allowed to come and play after school as he always has to go home and practise his musical instrument'

Different kinds of mummies

At the end of the day, no matter how friendly we are, and no matter how friendly the other mothers are, there are differences. Even if we don't want to admit it we do look at people and make judgements and compare ourselves to others.

Table 5 takes a light-hearted look at some of the different kinds of mummies you can find in the playground (apologies to the dads who do the school run for leaving you out of this section!).

Questionnaire 1 is for you to fill in if you want to explore this further.

Do you already recognise yourself as one kind or another? Or do you think a neat categorization is impossible?

The questionnaire led me to think about the people I had met and for me they can fall into four main themes. Table 6 shows these four possible themes and I have described them below:

Neat and tidy mummies

There are many women for whom being neat and tidy is important and who are keen for themselves and their families to look their best. These are the people who look good, and who are likely to have tidy homes and gardens. They are neat and tidy all year round and not just for special occasions! (I have always envied these mummies!).

Action mummies

These mummies are busy doing things. They often fill their time to capacity either at work or on committees or doing voluntary work. Their lives are full of activities. The children of action mummies are often very busy with out of school activities!

Earth mummies

These outdoor loving mummies may be referred to as Earth Mummies. They love being outdoors, and encourage their children to learn about nature. They are less interested in appearances and full on activities, and like to 'be' in the world. Camping, walking and being in the countryside are often their interests.

Struggling mummies

These are the mummies that sometimes have difficulties. They may suffer from anxiety and depression. They may have had difficulties in their own childhoods which make it difficult for them to be fully present for their families. Everyone experiences difficulties as they go through life but some people find it more difficult than others to cope with everyday problems; some people just have more to cope with. I know I have been a struggling mummy at times. Those mums with their own parents young enough to take on a significant amount of childcare have a very different life from a mum bringing up her children on her own with little outside support. This mother may also be a carer for her own parents.

Of course there is no definitive questionnaire that tells you who is who and as you can see by my answers to the questionnaire we can fall into different groups, and it is likely that we will fall into different groups during different times of our life. I was indeed much more interested in my appearance and being neat and tidy when I was in my 30s!

The difficulties of categorisation

When I wrote the questionnaire and then filled it in myself I was quite surprised to find I had ticked several boxes and not all on related themes. I have included my filled in questionnaire for your perusal. **It is actually impossible to categorise people into neat boxes.** For example I look quite a sensible and organised sort of person on the outside, but on the inside I sometimes feel stressed! So it could also be that someone who looks like a perfect mummy on the outside could be a struggling mummy on the inside.

Summary of Chapter 4

This chapter has focused on the very beginnings and what parents and children will feel as the start of the first day of school approaches. The chapter looks at how we make first impressions of people and how we will know if someone is like us or not. Meeting the mums and dads will provide us with the widest range of different people that we are ever likely to meet. No wonder it is quite a challenge! But it is exciting too if we enjoy meeting different people. This chapter also has a light-hearted look at the different kinds of people we are likely to meet and warns, too, of the impossibility of boxing people into categories.

In fact, what started out as a light-hearted look at the different mums in the playground, has given me an important lesson in life – it is impossible to categorise people into neat boxes!

Sue Jones

Table 5
Different kinds of Mummies

Kinds of Mummies	Description
Yummy Mummy	Pretty, sexy, young, smart (sadly not the Author these days!)
Pushy Mummy	Competitive with others. Sometimes opt for private education
Mumsie Mummy	Acutely child orientated and less interested in own activities and appearance
Disorganised Mummy	Often late, may not reply to party invites, disorganised with school forms and activities
Sister Mummy	Looks too young to be a Mummy (older mummies may feel envious!)
On the Committees Mummy	Enjoys being involved in all the school activities and committees. Sometimes had a high powered job before having children
Granny Mummy	The older Mummies sometimes mistaken for Grannies! (I found that rather annoying!)

Struggling Mummy	Children are not always at school. Needs school support and often unsupported at home
Accessory Mummy	'I love your new bag!' 'Where did you get that necklace?'
Organised Mummy	Always gives forms back the next day, very quick at replying to party invites. Children always send thank you notes
Earth Mummy	Loves nature and is passionate about recycling. May breastfeed for over a year
Stressy Mummy	A little on the edge (we've all been there!). May raise voice to children, may sometimes be in tears
Perfect Mummy	The Gold Standard! Practically perfect in every way!
Academic Mummy	Often likes to work towards qualifications and enjoys reading and going on courses. Often has high hopes for children
Scary Mummy	Unfriendly, may seem aloof

Action Mummy	Sporty Mummy with hardly a moment to spare in between activities. Children often involved in many activities
Busybody Mummy	Wants to know what everyone is up to!
Outdoor Mummy	Likes outdoor activities. May enjoy camping. Sometimes scout and guide leaders

Questionnaire 1
Different kinds of Mummies (for you to fill in)

Mummy Type	Always	Sometimes	Never
Yummy Mummy			
Pushy Mummy			
Mumsie Mummy			
Disorganised Mummy			
Sister Mummy			
On the committees Mummy			
Granny Mummy			
Struggling Mummy			
Accessory Mummy			
Organised Mummy			
Earth Mummy			
Stressy Mummy			
Perfect Mummy			
Academic Mummy			
Scary Mummy			
Action Mummy			
Busybody Mummy			
Outdoor Mummy			

If you could choose one kind of mummy, who would it be ?

Questionaire 1

Different kinds of Mummies (filled in by me)

Mummy Type	Always	Sometimes	Never
Yummy Mummy			✓
Pushy Mummy		✓	
Mumsie Mummy		✓	
Disorganised Mummy			✓
Sister Mummy			✓
On the committees Mummy			✓
Granny Mummy		✓	
Struggling Mummy		✓	
Accessory Mummy			✓
Organised Mummy		✓	
Earth Mummy	✓		
Stressy Mummy		✓	
Perfect Mummy			✓
Academic Mummy	✓		
Scary Mummy			✓
Action Mummy		✓	
Busybody Mummy		✓	
Outdoor Mummy		✓	

Table 6
Four possible themes of Mummies in the playground

Neat and Tidy Mummies	Earth Mummies
Yummy Mummy Sister Mummy Accessory Mummy Perfect Mummy	Earth Mummy Mumsie Mummy Granny Mummy Outdoor mummy
Action Mummies	**Struggling Mummies**
'On the committees' Mummy Pushy Mummy Academic Mummy Organised Mummy Busybody Mummy Action Mummy	Scary Mummy Disorganised Mummy Struggling Mummy Stressy Mummy

Chapter 5
The School Run

The school run is a unique activity that only parents with school age children are engaged in. Of course most people have heard of the term 'the school run', but before I had any children I had only been aware that there were more cars on the road in the morning during school term times.

So what is the school run?

The school run is a twice daily activity that is sometimes fun, sometimes stressful, and always relentless! For someone who is responsible for the school run all activities and work during the day must be geared around the school run. And there is little flexibility in timings because our little ones can't be late for school and they can't be left stranded at the end of the day with parents collecting them to suit their own schedules. Some people are lucky enough to have grandparents to help them but many are not.

The school run involves an outward journey to drop our children or child off at school and a homeward journey that collects our child and brings them safely home.

The school run also involves an interesting period of time – we, as parents, get to stand in the playground or close by the playground at the beginning of the day and at the end of the school day. We are not there for long - maybe 15-20 minutes at each end of the day. Surely nothing can happen in that short time? Can it?

But if we add the time up (taking 30 minutes per day), we will have spent 2 hours and 30 minutes in the playground each week and this adds up to 30 hours each school term and over a year approximately 90 hours! That is a lot of time for us, and as people tend to do, we fill this time with many different activities. Believe me, a lot can happen to us in that special playground time. Some of it lovely and some of it ghastly with all shades in between! But before we get into all that, let's look in a bit more detail at the two aspects of the school run.

The outward journey

This is a short case history to illustrate a possible morning:

Paula's story

I never seem to have enough time in the morning – we always seem to be in such a rush, and getting two children off to school is a strain. Sometimes there is even a bit of shouting! From actually sitting upright in bed, getting dressed in clean clothes, arriving at breakfast, eating something and not complaining about the type of yoghurt, brushing hair, making a plait for Lily, brushing teeth, washing face, finding shoes, getting school bag ready and finally getting out of the door can feel like achieving a marathon! Often I am going to work, and so I have to be reasonably smart and organise my own things too. Being a mum means you have to run your life, and those of your children, and there is nothing more difficult for me than getting us all out of the door on time! Add to this an argument between the children at breakfast time (for an example, my son may have touched my younger one's toast!) or a fancy dress day at school, and the school day starts with an extra edge. The most elaborate fancy dress day of all (and the school normally likes one a year!) was for all children in Year 1 to be dressed in a

Victorian outfit for a Victorian Day at school. Special days are fun when you get to school, but they do add a stress to the day's start.

We walk to school, which I feel is a good healthy start for the children. It is also a good time to try and practise spellings. Lily is more industrious than Jamie who is getting to the age when he is asserting himself and we have battles about spellings and even doing up his coat! Am I alone in this type of battle?

We arrive at school (on time!). Jamie goes to wait outside his class (he is in the upper school, and his class is around the back of the school) and I wait in the playground for Lily's teacher to come out and collect the children. I chat to the mothers of Lily's friends, and begin to relax after the rush. Sometimes we chat for longer after the line of children has gone into class – it is quite a social time. Little groups of mothers can be seen dotted about in the playground or just outside the school discussing this and that. When I don't need to go to work, I can chat for as long as I want, which is nice **as** I like to catch up with my friends in the morning.

The homeward journey

Karen's story looks at her homeward journey and also includes some detail on her children's after school activities.

Karen's story

I am the sort of person who doesn't like to be late; I guess I would describe myself as quite organised. I am usually one of the first mums to be standing waiting in the playground. Mums tend to join me as they arrive, so we chat about our day, the weather, homework, that sort of thing. If I know the mums well I will talk about more personal things (but I am always a bit careful about what I say in the playground!). The children from each class come out to a specific area in the playground, and I always see Ellie's teacher with her class come out from the form room. After Ellie has come out and I ask her how her day has been, we head home either on foot or by car if I have been lazy! Taking Thursday as an example – we go home and have about 30 minutes at home before we have to head back out to school to collect Jimmy from cross country club. I remember to check that he has brought all his clothes out with him, and so armed with his PE kit and all his school clothes, we head back to the car. Once at home we have half an hour to get a quick meal on the table before Ellie has to go to Brownies and later Jimmy goes to Scouts. Busy day on Thursday!

The good things and the bad things about the school run

Let's ask some of the mums and dads what they think. We'll start with the good things!

The good things about the school run

- Having a laugh with other people
- Seeing the same people each day
- Having a structure to the day
- I'd probably still be in my pyjamas at 10 am if I didn't have the school run!
- Having support when I had a problem with my child
- Having a good friend to talk to

- I enjoy seeing my children arrive at school happy and start playing with other children
- Waving them off as they go into school
- No-one understands motherhood like other mothers
- When things were difficult with my partner, it was the other mothers who really supported me
- Finding out about the school, the teachers and what's going on
- The gossip!

So much is positive about friendship and support, and the general well-being associated with sharing our lives with other parents, that I have dedicated a chapter to this area. **Chapter 6, Friendship and Support in the Playground** looks at friendships made on the school run. These friendships are unique and special, but they are fragile too.

So what about some of the difficult things associated with the school run? There seemed to be more difficulties that I expected.

Difficulties associated with the school run

- Feeling I need to wear something smart (and different) each day
- Feeling that I ought to chat and be friendly even when sometimes I felt a bit low
- Not always feeing included in the clique
- Having to see someone I had fallen out with
- Having to talk about boring things like housework!
- Doing the same thing day after day
- Feeling I was not as smart as some

- After I had had a difficulty with two of the mums I didn't know where to stand in the playground!
- I felt quite old compared to some of the others
- Standing around with a lot of people who were quite different from me
- Feeling awkward with another mother when I had told her of a difficulty my daughter had with hers (now they are best friends again!)
- Comparing myself to others

There seems to be two distinct areas of difficulty emerging from these comments.

One area relates to how we feel inside and relates to our self esteem. A lot of these difficulties stem from how we compare ourselves to others and how we cope when other people have different values from ourselves. Do we measure up? Do they measure up? Often nothing has happened – we just feel a bit paranoid!

Chapter 7, Paranoia in the Playground looks at these feelings. Although we may not want to admit to this, all of us compare ourselves to others and judge others based on our own value system. The feelings we get when we compare ourselves to others are sometimes uncomfortable and are more common that we would like to believe.

The second distinct area of difficulty comes when something does actually happen. Often, it would seem, outside of our control! Let's take, for example, the horror of our child being mean to another child. The interaction that may occur between you and the mother of the other child may not be comfortable. Worst still, if we are friends with the other mother, our friendship may be put under a severe strain. It may even finish the friendship. There is fragility in the relationships between parents if the children are friends, as it is never just a friendship between adults as it is in other areas of our lives, like in a work environment. Mother and child form an unbreakable bond which complicates friendships. **Chapter 8, Mother Tiger, Baby Cub (What affects you, affects me!)**, looks at how difficult relations between children can lead to difficult relations between parents. The unique thread between mother and child makes it impossible to stand separately in difficult situations. We can never be truly objective and are more than likely to stand on the side of our child (and as a child that is exactly what we want and need from our parents!).

Leaving these difficult situations for now, there are other school activities that will affect parents who are responsible for the school run.

Organising activities

Parents who are organising activities will use the playground time for networking. We will all, at some time, be involved with the following:

- Parties
- School events e.g. Summer fete or Christmas fair
- Social events
- Collections

Organising parties

Parties deserve a special mention, because they are fun and exciting for children! They also involve choice and with that inclusion and exclusion. The invites to parties are often given out in the playground. The child often gives them out under the watchful eye of mother (and sometimes under the watchful eyes of other mothers!). Don't be fooled into thinking that children (and mothers) don't know who is going to whose party.

Here is an example of mine to show what can happen.

In Year 2 my son wanted to invite all the girls in his class to his party but since there was a number restriction on the party venue, he could only invite half of the boys. About two days after the invites had gone out he began telling me that some of the boys were asking why they hadn't been invited. Not only that, my son was asking me why some of the boys hadn't been invited especially since one of them, as it turns out, was quite a good friend. At this stage I had hoped that those who had not been invited would not notice because at the end of the day not all children can go to all parties, but it felt awkward. It showed me clearly that even in Year 2, children are aware of what is going on, and they feel a level of acceptance and rejection. Chatting in the playground to the mum of a child you have not invited can feel very awkward indeed.

Similarly, if your child has not been invited to a party you do of course feel sad for your child (especially if they are upset) and if you are honest you might feel a tiny bit less friendly towards the mother organising the party. This is a normal reaction, no matter how maturely we tell ourselves that not everyone can be invited to all parties. It is also a good learning point, no matter how difficult, to begin learning that we are not chosen for everything.

Organising school events

The great organisers of school events are likely to use the playground as an arena for networking. These organisers may have had high profile jobs before they became 'just a mum'. They will arrive with maybe a clip-board and a few children in tow and before you know it, your name will be added to the growing list of 'willing' helpers. These organisers are a vital resource for the school as they are often the voluntary members of the committees that make extra money for the school e.g. organising the school fete or Christmas fair. Some of these mums may be a bit driven in their desire to get the job done, but they are a real asset and make a vital contribution to the school.

Organising social events

Well I suppose this is a bit like the party situation! At first when social events are organised it normally involves everybody, like an inclusive trip to the park or an inclusive night out for mums. All classes are different but each usually has a tradition of one night out for all the mums especially in the early years. Some classes carry this tradition on until the end of Primary school, while other classes seem to break up into smaller groups earlier. The feelings of inclusion or exclusion tend to mirror what happens for our children with regard to parties. We feel happy to be included and sad if we are not. I can remember a group of mums all setting off to Bluewater, with one of the mums driving, and as they all waved me off I wondered why I had not been invited!

Organising collections

Some schools have a tradition of organising collections for the teacher at Christmas and at the end of the year. In our school we tended to ask for a specific (small) amount of money and asked our children to write some words of relevance on a sticker which would then be entered into a card. I had done this at the end of the year, and although it seemed like a small job at first, it involved quite a lot of work trailing around the playground trying to collect money and stickers. Also it usually involved the short presentation when the present and card were handed over. Looking back, maybe having that clipboard would have made my life easier!

Summary

As we have seen, the school run involves two distinct aspects:

- An outward journey to drop off our child at school, and
- A homeward journey to collect our child from school

We stand in the playground for maybe 15 minutes at the beginning of the day and 15 minutes at the end of the day. A small amount of time on its own, until we add it up! Over a week we will have stood waiting for an average of 2 hours and 30 minutes but over seven years that adds up to approximately 630 hours!!

Table 7 gives some average times that we will have stood waiting for our children in, or near, that playground.

So much can happen in that huge amount of time. Some of it great (see Chapter 6) and some of it difficult (see Chapters 7 and 8).

What an extraordinary (and little known) experience the school run is!

Table 7
Number of hours mums/dads spend in or near the playground (average!)

Time period	Number of hours (average)
One day (2 runs)	30 minutes
Over a week (10 runs)	2 hours 30 minutes
Over a half term (6 weeks)	15 hours
Over a full term (12 weeks)	30 hours
Over a year (36 weeks)	90 hours
Over 7 years (Years R – 6)	630 hours (nearly 4 whole weeks!)

Sue Jones

Chapter 6
Friendship and Support in the Playground

For most mothers, the best thing about meeting other mothers in the playground is the friendship and support that develops over time.

Help and support bringing up our children

Meeting mothers in the playground provides us with an amazing pool of people. These people can offer us advice, support and friendship. Nothing is more important to us than providing a safe, secure and happy life for our children and having support for this extraordinarily important (and often little recognised!) job helps us enormously. The biggest and most difficult challenge for us is how best to bring up our children. If it is our first child we are inexperienced and friendship with other mothers offers us an invaluable support in this area as Jane's story illustrates:

Jane's story

When my first child started at Primary school I made friends with two mums whose first children were already at the school. They obviously had a lot of experience about the school and the way things were organised and it really helped me to hear about the school and to hear about what the teachers were like. It was also helpful to ask advice about really little things like whether to have school lunch or packed lunch, and how much I should worry about children catching nits – that sort of thing! But there was another thing that friendship with the school mums helped me with, and that was discussing and talking through how we brought up our children, how we got them to do what we wanted them to do (like eating vegetables –

no easy answer there!) and how to discipline them. What a difficult job it is to bring up children, but how helpful to be able to discuss our situation with other mums. Not everyone does the same thing but it is helpful to look at different options before choosing our own strategies. There is no qualification on 'How to be a mum' – we have to learn as we go along!

Help and support related to school life

As friendships deepen we learn to trust other people and begin to share other aspects of our life. We have any number of difficulties showered upon us in our life, some may be related to school life and others are related to life outside school.

We often experience some difficulties related to school life itself (although hopefully not too many). The following list, although by no means exhaustive, gives us some of the difficulties we may experience:

- Child not wanting to go into school
- Child not liking the teacher
- Child making friends with the 'naughty ones'
- Child not making friends easily
- Child falling out with best friend
- Child not wanting to do homework
- Child not wanting to wear his coat in the winter (my particular problem!)
- Child becoming more challenging as the years go by

...........and then there are a few others:

- Worrying about fancy dress costumes (my particular worry!)

- Deciding whether to go on outings with the class or not
- Deciding whether your child is too poorly to go to school
- Worrying about whether your children might catch nits (another worry of mine!)
- Deciding whether to help in the school

The list does go on and on if you are a worrying sort of person (you may now begin to guess that the Author may be of the worrying kind!).

Jenny's story illustrates how her friendship with Lynn supported her through her most difficult time with her daughter.

Jenny's story

My life with my daughter became really horrible in Year 2. My daughter, Olivia, suddenly decided that she was scared of her teacher. Olivia had been told off for something that she didn't feel had been all her fault and the teacher had seemed cross. Then for about two months Olivia didn't want to go into class. She cried each morning and clung to my hand like a limpet. The teaching assistant finally managed to take her in. I had talked to the teacher, who had said that Olivia was fine when she went into class, but I felt so bad watching her distress and wanted to take her home with me. While I watched in tears as she was taken into class, it was my friend Lynn who helped me though this time. Lynn was the mum of my daughter's friend and was always there to put an arm round me and talk to me. Sometimes we would go off and have coffee together. She was a huge support at a really horrible time, which luckily for all of us did not last all that long.

Help and support related to life events

Of course there are other difficulties in life that don't stem from school life, but these other difficulties can affect the life of our child at school and bring our family life into a difficult and sometimes chaotic place.

Some of these life events happen to all of us at one time or another, and at times like these we need support from our family and friends. Some examples of life events are listed as follows:

- Difficulty with partner
- Divorce
- Bereavement
- Illness, self or family member
- Elderly relatives needing care
- Redundancy
- Financial difficulties

The next mum, Nicola, illustrates the help she received from her friends during the illness and death of her father.

Nicola's story

Nothing prepared me for my father getting cancer and dying. Although he was in his eighties he had been quite fit until his diagnosis. The whole awfulness of it all quite took over my life. It was hard to focus on the children and other aspects of life at that time. I felt it was really hard to remember things, and looking back now, I think I was in quite an anxious state. My friend from the school, Ella, had lost her father-in-law a few years ago and was really sympathetic. She was happy to listen to me talk about my Dad, and seemed to understand what I was going through. Near the end of his life she was always happy to look after my two children if I needed to visit the hospital and she was a tremendous support when he eventually died and I had funeral arrangements to make. This was the saddest time of my life and the support Ella gave me helped to pull me through. I hope that one day I can be as supportive to her.

Strange phenomena of the playground friendships

I believe that adult friendships developed in the playground are unique. They are special, they are some of the closest friendships ever made, but they are fragile too. The following phenomena, I believe, are pertinent to the friendships formed in the playground:

Transient friendships

Friendships can move on in a way that is not experienced elsewhere. Friendships between mothers often develop when one child is friendly with another. Almost all of my close friendships developed as a result of my children's friendships. But to my surprise, some of these friendships did not outlast the children's friendships! For example, friendships made at school, may not continue as the children move on through to Secondary school. As the children go their separate ways, so do some of the friendships made between us. There are many things that cement a friendship, but if it is just the friendship of the children then this will not survive when the children are no longer friends.

As our second children start Primary school, a whole new group of friends are made, and it is not uncommon for mothers to spend more time in the playground with their younger children. After all, as the children get older, they are more independent, and so often prefer to go into school and come out of school on their own. In fact, parents may not be encouraged to wait in the playground outside the classes for children in Years 5 and 6 in order to encourage this independence.

The friendships of our children evolve and in a parallel manner, so do our friendships with the mothers. Patty's story gives an illustration of this.

Patty's story

In the first year of Primary school, my little boy was very friendly with another boy, and I became friendly with his mum, Georgie. She was easy to talk to and fun to be with and as we both had younger children not yet at Primary school, we started to see each other a lot, taking the children to the same activities and always having tea together at each other's houses on a Wednesday afternoon. It was good fun and I felt our friendship was strong. However, because her second child was one year older than my second child, he started school a year sooner. And then to my surprise, I hardly saw her! Obviously we couldn't do the same activities with the younger children now that her youngest had started school, but even the teas stopped! It took me a while to notice that Georgie was now great friends with mums from her youngest child's class at school and it felt as if she had dropped me for them. I felt quite sad for a while, but have now realised that the children were all that we had in common..

Friendships are never independent

The friendship between you and the mother of your child's best friend is never an independent one. It is 'as if' the relationship is paired.

Diagram 3 illustrates this pairing. If our friendship is based on an initial friendship between our children, the friendship can rarely be independent.

Nothing is nicer than seeing our children make friends. Nothing is nicer than sharing our happiness with the mother of our child's friend! Friendships between children and mothers are forged quickly and a bond like no other develops.....until the friendship between our children falter. Never let it be said that we are not affected by our children's pain. Friendships between mothers can end as quickly as they are born, if the children fall out in a big way!

This strange and unique phenomenon is described in full detail in **Chapter 8, Mother Tiger, Baby Cub (What affects you affects me!)**.

Friends make other friends

It is obvious that people are going to make different friends and we can't keep our favourite person all to ourselves. However sometimes our new friends make friends with someone they didn't previously like. Maybe you have spent some time gossiping about this person, and now your friend and this person are becoming friends. It is 'as if' we are in Primary school ourselves!

However this is not an uncommon situation as the following story illustrates.

Jilly's story

Well I feel really anxious about this one. I had been friends with Marie for ages. Our children were in the same form and were good friends. We often helped each other out with the school run and journeys to parties and both our girls were in Brownies. There was one mum from our girls' class who had irritated us both, she was quite outspoken and said just what was on her mind! It was an unspoken agreement between us that she was not 'our sort' of person. Imagine my surprise when my friend Marie had said that this lady had asked one morning if she had wanted to have a coffee and my friend had gone along. I was expecting her to say the usual things and tell me what a pain this mother had been. But no! She said 'Actually she isn't that bad when you get to know her!'. I could not believe it! Over the following months my friend met this lady now and again and then I found out that Marie and her partner were going out with this mum and her husband. Stupid as it sounds, I felt really left out! But worse, were all the things we'd discussed and said about this mum. I felt I couldn't trust Marie any more. What would she talk about to this other mum - the mum I still didn't like? Would she tell her some of the things I had said? Were they now talking about me? Was I soon to be marginalised? Or had that already happened? Sadly I am not sure if my friendship with Marie will be the same again.

And finally, and this is a warning, the playground is a fertile ground for gossip!

Gossip

The playground really is a hotbed of gossip and news and although it can be very interesting to hear about what is going on for others, it is important to choose wisely who you tell things to as what goes around can come back to us.

If there is one word of advice I should give it would be to **choose carefully what you say about other people, and choose carefully who you say it to**. You never know when or if it will be passed on.

Summary

This chapter summarises how the friendships born from the school run can help us out in all sorts of situations. The friendships with other mothers are very special, but can be fragile too.

The short stories that have been included illustrate how friendship is invaluable and provides support in many different situations including:

- Situations relating to school life (e.g. child not wanting to go into school, child not liking the teacher etc), and
- Situations relating to life events (e.g. difficulty with partner, bereavement, illness, redundancy etc).

Sometimes it is only the friendship and support of our friends that gets us through these really tough times. I know that when my father became ill after having had a stroke when he was in his nineties, it was the support of the other mums that helped me get through this really tough patch in my life.

In this chapter we also touch on the shadow side of our friendships, and this will be discussed more in the next two chapters.

Diagram 3

Relationship pairing between mother and child

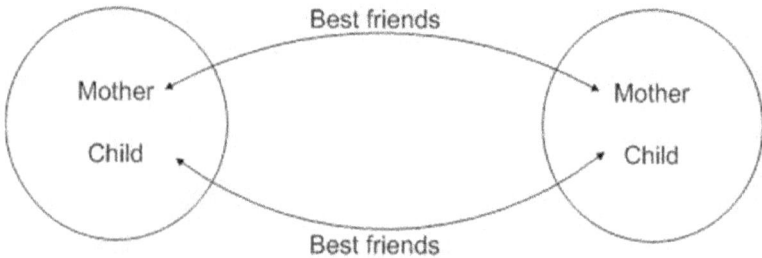

Best friends

Mother

Child

Mother

Child

Best friends

Chapter 7
Paranoia in the Playground

Chapter 6, Friendship and Support in the Playground, looks at the best things about our interactions with other mothers. However there are some negative aspects to this huge amount of exposure to other people, as comments from these mums indicate:

Examples of common paranoia!

'I just couldn't believe it when this mum started telling me who were the brightest children in my daughter's class; apparently the children were grouped by ability. I didn't know this. Needless to say her son was on the top table and my daughter wasn't!'

'Some days I just felt exhausted while taking Toby to school. What with recently having a new baby and not getting much sleep, it seemed a marathon effort to get Toby to school on time. I always felt a bit of a mess as I raced to school with Toby and Chloe in her pram, and I was always aware of how well put together some of the mums were - so neat and tidy! I was beginning to wonder just how long they had to get ready in the morning!'

'I couldn't understand why Frannie hadn't been invited to her friend's party. Most of the children seemed to be going and Frannie was really sad. The other mum seemed to be ignoring me too. This surprised me (and hurt my feelings) as we had been talking a lot in the playground. But worse was how Frannie had taken it.'

'Not long after Lydia started school I made friends with a mum who had a little boy the same age as my second child. We used to have coffee together on a

Tuesday, taking it in turn to go to each other's houses. It wasn't long before I noticed that this mum's house was always spotless, and mine was not! I started to tidy and clean before she came over, the whole thing became rather a chore.'

'I feel bad saying this, but I felt really uncomfortable picking my child up from this birthday party. The mum was smoking when she answered the door, and it seemed as if she had had a couple of glasses of wine. She was really friendly and everything, but it didn't feel right for a children's party.'

'I always felt pressurised to do some voluntary work for the school. However it's not easy for me as I have to look after my mother as well. Lots of these ladies on the committees have young grandparents who help them out a lot. I don't expect they realise how lucky they are.'

'When I gave back a t-shirt to a friend (who had leant it to me for Josie during a paddling pool afternoon) I gave it in an ordinary grocery plastic bag. However, when she gave me something, a few months later, she used a smart designer bag from her clothes shopping! And she wasn't the only one. You will think I'm silly, but I then started collecting my smart bags for use in the school playground!'

'I always make an effort to look nice when I go and pick up Charlie. It astonishes me that some people don't seem to bother at all. Some people's standards are very different from mine!'

'I dashed shopping before school pick up and arrived at the playground with at least 6 shopping bags hooked over my buggy. Do you know at least five mums made a comment and seemed to find it amusing? It was the last time I did that, and I never spotted anyone else with a lot of shopping hanging from their buggies! It was almost as if it was an unspoken rule to keep all bags of grocery shopping out of the playground. Maybe bags of clothes would have received a different response!'

'I was really friendly with this mum when my little girl first started at Primary school, but after a few terms I noticed that the mum was talking to me less and to some of the other mums much more! I felt really awkward. Had I done something wrong? Had she got fed up with me? Had she just moved on to a new set of friends?'

'I always seem to be standing near some mums who look fabulous. One of them is even a cordon bleu chef! I haven't seen inside any of their houses, but I am sure they are immaculate!'

Four areas of paranoia

Reading through the previous examples, we can see that paranoia in the playground can be caused by four different areas:

- Comparison and supposed pressure from others
- Relationship changes
- What's wrong with my child?
- Playground norms

The first area is a very interesting topic that affects all our daily lives to some degree, although as we will see, some people are more susceptible to uncomfortable feelings related to comparison than others.

Comparison and supposed pressure from others

It can be seen from the previous examples that a lot of the anxiety that can occur by certain interactions is related to comparison with others. These comparisons can take many forms, can set up feelings of unease and unfortunately are prevalent in all aspects of our lives, not just in the school playground!
So what are these comparisons in the playground?

- How we look
- How our children look
- How our house and front garden look
- How bright our children are
- What activities our children do
- How many friends our children have
- How happy our children seem
- What other mums do
- How helpful we are to the school

How perfect life would be for me if I always had a tidy house and front garden! How perfect life would be if my children (and myself of course!) looked neat and tidy. How good it would feel if my children were top of the class and happy and popular to boot. How marvellous I would feel if I could cook nourishing dinners every night and have plenty of time to help out at the school. I could then stand in the playground and feel truly on top of everything. I would be Super Mum!!

The reality of life

Let's do a little questionnaire and I will share with you the realities of my life. Questionnaire 2 shares my answers with you. It is difficult to get all ticks in the 'Good' column (although I am sure there are people who will). In fact looking at this questionnaire, I can see that the people who I compare myself to the most (and find myself lacking) are the people who would score a 'Good' in the areas I would tick 'Room for Improvement'. The mums I feel most daunted by are those that look great and whose houses and front gardens are neat (I fear that these people are often good cooks too!!). Now I have shared my particular paranoia with you, it is time for you to be brave and fill in your own questionnaire. Questionnaire 2 is also for you to fill in.

So why do we compare ourselves to others?

This is quite a difficult question to answer. If comparing ourselves to others sets up uncomfortable feelings we can ask ourselves why do we do it? After all, we are all different and what is acceptable to one person is not always acceptable to another. We all have our own set of family values which are passed down from one generation to another. Each family has its own set of values which create differences between families.

We have touched on life values in Chapter 4, but the following examples will give an example of where differences between families may occur:

Life values of Family 1

- It is important to be reasonably well turned out
- It is important to look after things
- It is important to follow fashion
- It is important to keep things tidy
- It is important to look our best
- It is important to do things to the best of our ability
- Details are important

Looking at these life values you can see how different this family is from Family 2.

Life values of Family 2

- It is important to get involved in activities
- It is important to keep learning new things
- It is important to travel
- It is important to keep an eye on the big picture not the details
- It is important to try out new things
- I doesn't matter too much if we are a bit untidy

I have made these two families very different for the illustration in this book. Probably most of us have a mixture of the two. But for the sake of learning about values we can see that the two families illustrated are very different. It is easy to see that bringing people together from these two families may (but not always) make them both feel awkward because of these differences. Sometimes (but not always) it is easier to be with someone who has similar life values.

What might the mum from Family 1 think of the mum from Family 2

A mum with family values of the first family may look at the mum from Family 2 and think one of three things:

1. Why is she always rushing about doing all those things when she never has the time to tidy her house or dress her children neatly?
2. That mum is always involved in some activity, I wonder if I do enough?
3. That mum is very different from me, but she is really friendly and I don't think our differences will affect our friendship. I might even join her on one of her activities!

What might the mum from Family 2 think of the mum from Family 1?

Again there may be three different scenarios:

1. Do they do anything else but shopping and cleaning their house?!
2. She always looks fantastic and her front garden is perfect, I wonder where I am going wrong?
3. That mum is quite different from me but she is really friendly and her beautiful garden has inspired me to tidy mine up a bit!

The three scenarios

As you can see from the above examples there are three distinct scenarios which will relate to how we feel in the world at that particular time. They are as follows:

The better than you scenario

The first of the three comments from both the mums comes from the 'I feel better than you' position. This will set up comfortable (if not very kind) feelings of superiority!

The worse than you scenario

The second of the comments from the two mums comes from the 'I feel worse than you' scenario. This will set up uncomfortable feelings of inferiority. If we are going to feel paranoia in the playground then this is the life position we are starting from.

We are different but that's OK scenario

The third set of comments celebrates our differences and neither person feels superior or put down. We are different and that's ok. Obviously this is the most mature position, but not the easiest!

It would be great if we were all as grounded as the mums who make the third set of comments, but most of us compare ourselves to others and feel judgemental about those differences at least some of the time.

Eric Berne (1910-1970) who was the founder of Transactional Analysis described these scenarios as life positions. A simplified version of these is illustrated in Table 8. The table illustrates the different life positions that we find ourselves in and everyone will probably have a preferred life position but will move through all four positions now and again. I know that I try very hard to stay in the grounded 'we are different but that's OK scenario', but very often if I feel a bit untogether I can begin to find myself slipping into a horrible feeling of inadequacy, where I do not feel OK. Likewise, I have occasionally been known to feel a bit superior (not that I find this as easy to admit!).

The very worst scenario

You will notice that there is another quadrant in the table that has not been mentioned before – it is the quadrant where someone may feel 'I am hopeless and so are you'. This is a very negative position to reach and is quite a depressing position to be in, where the world and yourself and others are in a bleak place. I expect most of us have touched this place at one time or another.

If you are interested in reading more about Eric Berne, Transactional Analysis and the life positions he describes, I would recommend the following reference: Stuart, I and Joines, V. TA Today. Lifespace (2012).

Relationship changes

Looking back to the beginning of the chapter we highlighted four areas that seem to come up time and time again. Comparison and pressure from others is such a big topic that we have spent a fair amount of time talking about this area, but it is not the only area that causes us to feel anxious and a bit paranoid!

Another area that causes us mums some feelings of discomfort is when our relationship with other mums change in a mysterious (to us!) way.

Remember the comment from the start of the chapter:

'I was really friendly with this mum when my little girl first started at Primary school, but after a few terms I noticed that the mum was talking to me less and to some of the other mums much more! I felt really awkward. Had I done something wrong? Had she got fed up with me? Had she just moved on to a new set of friends?'

We know that something is different, but we don't know why. Sometimes it doesn't matter to us if we are less friendly with someone over time (after all a lot of friendships move on), but sometimes it does matter. It can become quite awkward when we are standing in the playground both in the morning and in the afternoon.

So what should we do in this situation? Well I don't think that there is a right or wrong answer. We can of course choose form the following options:

- Ask the mum if anything is wrong
- Accept it as a situation that may change again in the future
- Say nothing, but guess and guess what went wrong

The mum in the example was asking herself questions, and perhaps if you are brave and need an answer then asking what has happened can help. But there is a risk here; we may not end up with the answer we want, and we may not end up with the truth. Sometimes it is better to let things be, but accept that some difficulties with relationships are inevitable and that some people like to change their relationships regularly while other people like to make and keep their friends. Of course this is also very good practise for helping our children through the minefield of their own friendships. What a surprise to find that we are often going through exactly what our children are going through. It is as if we are back in Primary school ourselves!

What's wrong with my child?

This is another situation that we have already talked about a bit in **Chapter 5, The School Run.** This situation is one which we have all probably encountered at one time or another. Remember the example from the beginning of this chapter:

'I couldn't understand why Frannie hadn't been invited to her friend's party. Most of the children seemed to be going and Frannie was really sad. The other mum seemed to be ignoring me too. This surprised me (and hurt my feelings) as we had been talking a lot in the playground. But worse was how Frannie had taken it.'

It is very difficult not to feel some emotion when our children are left out of something and they feel upset. Even if they don't seem to mind too much, we are often left wondering why they haven't been invited. Of course children can't be invited to every event or birthday party on offer, but it is normal to feel for our children if they are not included in something they would have liked to have been.

On the other hand it can also become a bit of a headache holding a party. You can't invite everyone, there are children you feel you should invite and there are the children your child wants to invite (after all it is their party, although sometimes I have wondered...!). Invariably, unless you are inviting the whole class, some children will be left out. There will be the fun (and awkwardness!) of handing out the invitations, hoping that those not invited did not notice. Then there is the anxiety of standing near to the mums of children not invited and hoping they haven't noticed. Handing out the invites can be a bit of a stress all by itself, and all this is before the actual event!

Inviting small numbers for tea can cause just as many difficulties as then the small number indicates those that are special.

Chapter 8, Mother Tiger, Baby Cub (What affects you, affects me!), looks at the awkwardness of parties in greater depth and looks at why we feel the emotions our children feel. Suffice to say for the moment, the problem of parties can leave us a bit stressed out!

Playground norms

This is the funny one and always makes me chuckle! Remember these two examples from the beginning of the chapter:

'When I gave back a t-shirt to a friend (who had leant it to me for Josie during a paddling pool afternoon) I gave it in an ordinary grocery plastic bag. However, when she gave me something, a few months later, she used a smart designer bag from her clothes shopping! And she wasn't the only one. You will think I'm silly, but I then started collecting my smart bags for use in the school playground!'

'I dashed shopping before school pick up and arrived at the playground with at least 6 shopping bags hooked over my buggy. Do you know at least five mums made a comment and seemed to find it amusing? It was the last time I did that, and I never spotted anyone else with a lot of shopping hanging from their buggies! It was almost as if it was an unspoken rule to keep all bags of grocery shopping out of the playground. Maybe bags of clothes would have received a different response!'

There are definitely some unspoken playground norms to each and every school. Each school will be different. Our playground norms were as follows:

- No smoking in the playground

- Look reasonably neat and tidy

- Always put on a bright face

- No bags of shopping (really!)

- Use of smart bags between mums (hilarious!)

All schools will have their own norms (just as all groups do), and I believe the norms will represent the area the school is located in. No prizes for guessing that our norms came from middle class suburbia! It would be interesting to see what norms develop in the country, or in private schools or in inner city schools.

Summary

So in summary this chapter has explored these four areas:

- Comparison and supposed pressure from others
- Relationship changes
- What's wrong with my child?
- Playground norms

Paranoia in the playground can probably affect all of us to a certain degree. A lot of our uncomfortable feelings come from the comparisons we make with others, but other areas that can make life uncomfortable relate to changing relationships, all the anxieties relating to parties, not to mention learning the group norms for the playground!

And we thought it would be our children who would find it difficult at Primary school!

Questionnaire 2
Areas of playground comparison
(for you to fill in)

Comparison	Good	OK	Room for improvement
How I look			
How my children look			
Front garden			
House			
How bright my children are			
Happiness of children			
Activities of children			
Help to the school			
Cooking skills			
How many friends our children have			
My own activities/job			

Questionnaire 2
Areas of playground comparison
(filled in by me!)

Comparison	Good	OK	Room for improvement
How I look		✓	
How my children look		✓	
Front garden			✓
House			✓
How bright my children are		✓	
Happiness of children	✓		
Activities of children	✓		
Help to the school		✓	
Cooking skills			✓
How many friends my children have		✓	
My own activities/job	✓		

Table 8
The four scenarios (or life positions)

Grounded	Inferior/paranoid
I'm OK and so are you! Best scenario.	**You are OK, but I am not!** You are better than me.
Superior	**Hopeless**
I'm OK but you are not! I'm definitely better than you.	**I'm not OK and neither are you!** The very worst scenario.

Sue Jones

Chapter 8
Mother Tiger, Baby Cub
(What affects you, affects me!)

Mother Tiger protects her cub at all cost in the jungle. Nothing will stand in her way. Nothing is different standing here in the playground! Mothers, too, will protect their children at all costs including their friendships between themselves and other mothers. The playground can change from being a friendly and sociable place to a scary and intimidating place for us mothers!

This chapter looks at several interesting and interconnecting phenomena including:

- Developing empathy between mother and child
- What affects you, affects me (the small stuff)
- What affects you, affects me (the big stuff)
- The link between parent and child – the dyadic unit
- The parallel process
- Why friendships between mothers can be so precarious

Developing empathy between mother and child

The bond between mother and child is so great that often when our children are hurting, we feel that hurt too.

Empathy begins to develop between mother and child at the confirmation of pregnancy (when we begin to think of our new baby and how our life will now change). At birth we start to learn and anticipate the needs of our new baby. Does that fearsome cry mean he is hungry or does it mean that he is not pleased to be put down in his carry cot?

As babies grow and become toddlers their interactions with us become more complex, and all the time the new mother is trying to understand her child's communication and to interpret the needs of her growing infant. With the development of basic speech and the ever growing sophistication of socialization, mother and child are usually bonded and the mother has a deep empathy for her child. Obviously this is not always the case and some parents don't feel such empathy for their child, and some mother and baby pairings don't fit together as well as some others. Some mothers may not have the time or energy to bond with their children and in these situations a firm attachment with deep empathy is unlikely to be formed.

Obviously all mums are different and some will be more empathic than others, but happily in most cases, mother and child develop as a well bonded unit. Luckily, in most cases, by the time our children reach Primary school we are pretty much in tune with what our children like and what they don't like. We know what makes them sad or angry, excited or anxious.

What affects you affects me (the small stuff)

We care so much about our children that the things that make them sad, often make us sad too, and the things that annoy them can make us annoyed too. Here are some examples of how the feelings of our children, affected the feelings of their mothers:

'His new friend at school started playing with another child. He was so sad. I felt so sad for him that I had a pain in my chest!'

'Another child took his best pencil with the special rubber. He was really cross and almost in tears with disappointment. I felt like going up to that child and searching his pencil case – I felt that cross!'

'My child's seat was next to the window which made him very hot and uncomfortable in the summer. I spent a lot of time feeling hot myself, and worrying about whether he would remember to take off his jumper!'

'In his first year he wasn't invited to this boy's birthday party to which a lot of classmates were invited. He felt sad and left out. I did too and wondered why he hadn't got an invitation. However he didn't play with this child a lot, and I explained to him that sometimes we have to make choices, and that we can't be invited to all the parties. I tried to be very grown up about this but I could also feel his disappointment.'

There are many other examples that I can think of from my own children's time at Primary school. Some are relatively small events that we can help our children come to terms with as the last example shows.

However, there are other events that can happen that can bring parents into conflict. Let us never underestimate the wrath of Mother Tiger. As mothers we all have a Mother Tiger tucked inside ready to protect our cub!

What affects you, affects me (the big stuff)

One of the things that took me by surprise about my friendships with other mothers was the unbreakable link between them and their children. Of course this was obvious when I thought about it, but what wasn't so obvious was that the state of my friendship with another mother rather depended on what was going on with our children. Mums have marvellous relationships while their children are getting on. There is nothing more pleasing than seeing your child play with another, and for another child to really like your child, especially when they first start school. How warm and cosy everything is! How well the children are getting on. How warm and friendly our relationship is with the other mum. But what happens when things go wrong between the children and difficulties occur? The following stories illustrate some of these difficulties:

Eva's story

My daughter had been really friendly with another girl for several years, and they had always seemed happy playing together. But then suddenly, out of the blue, my daughter was not invited to her friend's birthday party and she was really upset. I felt really upset for her and felt annoyed with the other mother for leaving her out. In fact I bravely rang her up and asked why. Apparently, the other mother told me, our children had been developing different friendship groups over the year, but I was not aware of this. We had been friends before this happened but I was cross afterwards and I didn't feel like being so friendly for a while.

Sandra's story

My daughter was friendly with two other girls who were in the same class. I know they say 'three is a difficult number' but they seemed to get on and over the years they had many happy times together and the three of us mums got on really well and had even been on a minibreak together. Then in Year 5 something really difficult began to happen and my daughter started getting left out of arrangements. She was upset about it so I spoke to the other mums. They didn't really want to talk about it at first, but then said that they thought my daughter had been upsetting the other two! Well, as you can imagine, I felt upset and angry about this and I felt betrayed by the other mothers. In fact I felt exactly what my daughter was feeling about her friendships! After a few months my daughter made other friends and that was a relief. But what happened to my friendship with the other mothers? The friendship just seemed to peter out. However, like my daughter, I was also beginning to make new friends.

Jenny's story

My daughter had been very friendly with another girl while she had been at preschool and they were pleased to find out that not only were they going to the same 'big' school, they were also going to be in the same class. However my child began to make other friends in her new class and the other child was upset at first.....and so was her mother! She kept letting me know that my child wasn't so close now to her child. I felt bad for her, but there was not much I could do. I wasn't in class to see what was happening. In the end her child made other friends and often the children would play in a big group together. After the initial difficulty my relationship with this mum became easier. Luckily my daughter was having an easier time!

The above examples are not the little ups and downs of school life that will always occur between children. When a small upset occurs it is often in our best interest to help our children make up (when our children are little it is often easier for us to intervene and help the children understand what is going on and to say sorry if necessary). However, it is when things change and seem to go badly wrong as the above examples illustrate, friendships (for both children and adults) can be irreversibly damaged.

In the examples given above the mothers' friendship was dependent on the situation with their children – no one felt pleased with the friendship after the upset between the children! The mothers' friendship in these examples was never independent of their children.

No matter how mature we like to think we are, it is almost impossible (if you have a close relationship with your child) for us not to feel what our children are feeling. If our child feels angry and upset towards another child, then it is often the case that we, too, will feel angry and upset. If the situation is so bad that the children are no longer friends then it is likely that we will feel unfriendly towards the mother who was our friend. How uncomfortable and upsetting all this is – rather like being back at school! Of course, how we react to the other mother may not be as extreme as completely ignoring them, there could be just a period of cooling off, but whatever happens to the friendship it is upsetting for children and parents alike.

Link between parent and child and the dyadic unit

Diagram 3 at the end of Chapter 6 shows the relationship pairing between mother and child and illustrates that when the children are happy together then so are the mothers. However when the children fall out in a big way then often the parents fall out as well. Diagram 4 illustrates this. In some unique way the parent/child dyad works as one unit, and so when there is great friendship between the children there is often a great friendship between the parents. However when the children fall out in a big way (and here I am not talking about the inevitable small upsets that always happen along the way), and there is a major upset, it is quite likely that the parents will have difficulties as well.

This was the one area of playground phenomena that I had not been prepared for and the most difficult thing is that it is totally out of our control! There is not much we can do to influence how our children develop friendships and the developing and breaking of friendships is one of the things that we learn in Primary school. It is a difficult area because although we don't want our children to upset other children and hope that we teach them how to behave in a kindly way towards others, we don't necessarily want our children to just stay friends with another child because the other child would be upset if other friends were made.

I am afraid that the whole area of making and breaking friendships is a minefield! And we as parents have little control about what goes on in school. I believe that it is inevitable that some upset and difficulties will occur and it is up to us as parents to be good role models to our children. If we get very angry and start a big old shouting match in the playground with another mother it does not give our children a good role model to follow! However it is true to say that fights between parents have occurred in the playground due to problems between children.

The parallel process

The parallel process is another way of looking at this strange situation. A parallel process (a term often used in the counselling arena), can be described as a process which is a mirror of the central situation. In the counselling arena it can be illustrated as something that might happen between counsellor and client (for example a feeling of anxiety) that is then mirrored in the relationship between counsellor and supervisor. A feeling of anxiety between supervisor and counsellor may indicate a central anxiety in the counselling room between counsellor and client. It is not just feelings that are mirrored, behaviour can be mirrored too. Taking the counselling situation again, a client may always be late for her session, and this behaviour may then be mirrored in supervision. The counsellor then may start to be late for supervision. It is difficult to know exactly why this sort of thing happens, but it does involve our unconscious processes which govern our life more than we may like!

If we leave the counselling room and return to the playground, we can see that the parallel process can occur between children and parents. The parallel process is mirrored in the parent's relationship and repercussions of this even reach our outer circle of friends, which may start to take sides if the damage to the relationship is severe. Those unconscious forces are at work whether we like them or not.

Diagram 5 aims to illustrate the parallel process that happens between children and parents and maybe even extending to an outer circle of friends.

Regression

But is there more going on than the unique relationship between parent and child, and the phenomenon called the parallel process? It is likely that another important phenomenon is at work when parents fall out in a big way. If the parents are beginning to feel childlike in some way, and maybe even feel that they are back at school themselves, then it is likely that something called regression is at work.

Regression can be described as a process when we begin to lose touch with our adult place and begin to feel like a child again. It can feel quite scary but sometimes it can feel quite powerful too. It will all depend on our own unique childhood and how we felt as a child. When we feel passionately about what our children are feeling, it is possible that some of us will lose touch with our own adult self. We have moved out of our grown-up place and into a more childlike place. It is possible that at this point we may start to behave like children in the playground as the following section illustrates.

What does all this mean in the jungle of the playground?

It means we have to be careful!   The following examples show situations that might happen which indicate that the three phenomena of the unique dyad, the parallel process and regression may be at work together. Parents will do unexpected things to protect their children.

- Where it might be best to let the children work out their own difficulties, parents may start to intervene with the friendship groups as if they are part of it.
- Parents may phone each other and have a go at each other, even though there is little anyone can do about the friendship groups as the children get older.
- Parents have been known to shout and have rows in the playground.

- Parents have been known (though rarely) to fight in the playground.
- Friends that once stood side by side, now stand at opposite ends of the playground – friends no more.
- Sad letters may be sent, hoping that friendships between parents and children may be rekindled
- Parents may feel that they have to take sides.
- Parent friendship groups may be divided if the children's' friendship groups are broken.

Never let it be said that grown-ups do not regress in the arena of the playground. When we hurt for our children, we will go to extraordinary lengths to either make things better or to punish those we perceive as responsible for their hurt. Although all of this may sound a bit dramatic, it is useful to be aware that we will meet Mother Tiger. We will meet Mother Tiger in ourselves and we will meet Mother Tiger in others. Let's not be too hard on ourselves or on other mothers as we, and they, only have the interests of Baby Cub in mind, even if some of the behaviour that we exhibit is not always helpful to our children!

Diagram 4

The dyadic unit of mother and child at work

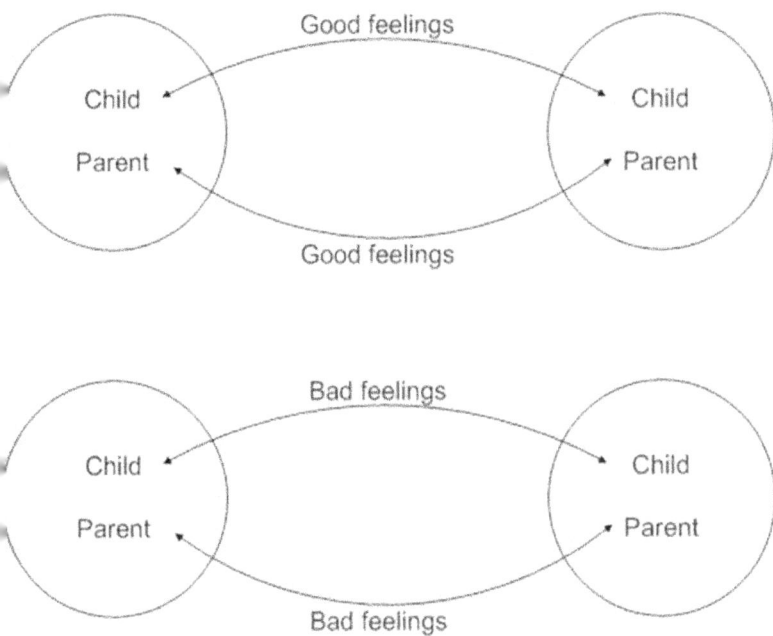

Good feelings

Child

Parent

Child

Parent

Good feelings

Bad feelings

Child

Parent

Child

Parent

Bad feelings

Diagram 5

Diagram of the parallel process

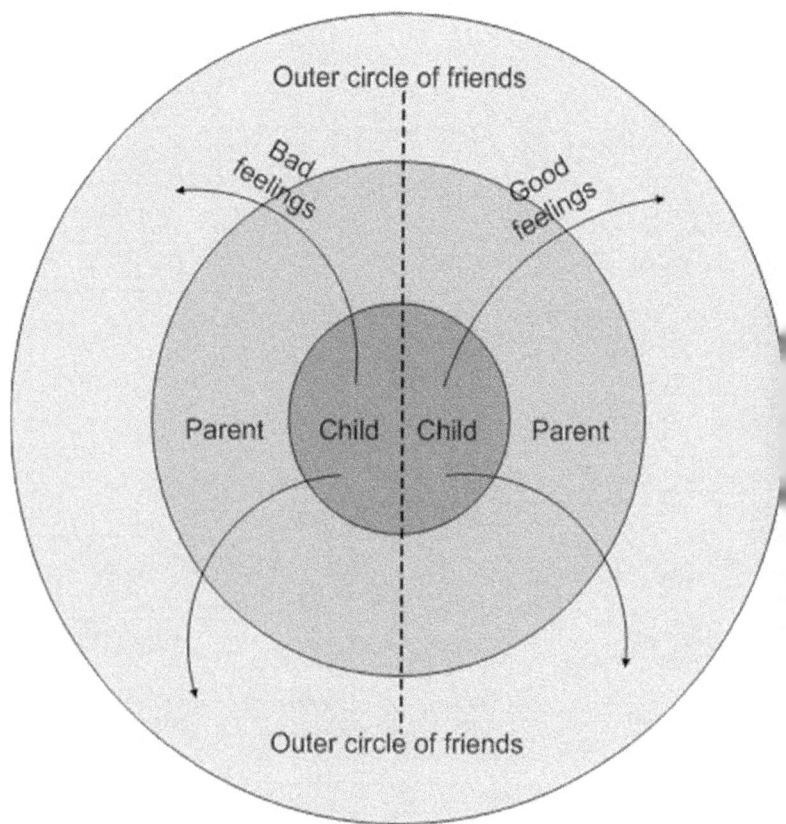

Outer circle of friends

Bad feelings

Good feelings

Parent | Child | Child | Parent

Outer circle of friends

Summary

Sue Jones

Chapter 9
Beginnings, Endings and Learning for all

This chapter aims to summarise all that we have learnt over the Primary school years and looks at how this prepares us for the next big step – Secondary school. I have purposely written 'us' here, as it is not just our child who is preparing for this next big transition in life.

This Chapter covers the following areas:

- Summary of what our children gain from playing in the playground
- Summary of what parents experience in the playground
- Endings at school and celebrations of a new beginning
- Loss for parents
- Secondary school
- The life of work – groups and organisations
- My top 10 tips of advice!
- Celebrating motherhood
- Final comments from the Author

Summary of what our children gain from playing in the playground

Hopefully you will have realised by now the importance of playgrounds and the chance to play at break and lunchtime. It is not just about getting fresh air and a chance to exercise to release the pent up energy and tension from sitting and concentrating – it is about much more.

It is, of course, very important that children do exercise and wear themselves out a bit as this will enable them to sit still and concentrate in lessons. From a personal point of view I am very much against keeping children in the classroom as a punishment for bad behaviour as it will just exacerbate the problems of fidgetiness and disruptiveness. Children who seem persistently annoying and disruptive may have ADHD and actually can't help their behaviour. These children are often punished if they are undiagnosed when in actual fact they may be tying their best. These are the children who need our help the most.

At playtime children get fresh air and time to exercise, but they gain much more than that. They have fun most of the time, they develop friendships, and through all this playing and having fun they are developing their social skills. These social skills are the building blocks of socialization.

Even from the very beginning babies are learning to communicate and socialize and these skills develop at home and at preschool. At Primary school children generally arrive with some well defined social skills and are ready to make friends. They generally know how to behave in a group. These skills are further developed as they go through Primary school. Children learn how to be a friend; not just being with another child but learning to be a good friend. They begin to learn how to deal with difficult situations and there is no better place for learning this than in the playground. As mothers we don't want our children to suffer any difficulties and disagreements but I do firmly believe that some small difficulties help us to negotiate life as we get older.

When we become adults and look for work we need to be able to use our advanced social skills of cooperation, negotiation and empathy. We develop different levels of competence at these and empathy is particularly difficult for children who are on the Autistic Spectrum. However these children may become brilliant scientists or mathematicians. It is lucky that we are all different.

These advanced social skills are all developing and practised in the playground. As mentioned before, because the playground is largely an unstructured part of the child's day, there are more opportunities for some difficulties and therefore some opportunities to practise these skills.

The playground is indeed a very important part of our children's development.

Summary of what parents experience in the playground

Such joy, such fun, such good friendships, such a stress, such a nightmare!

You may wonder what inspired me to write this book. I think it was because I had experienced a whole range of feelings - sometimes it was fun, sometimes it was supportive, sometimes I felt a mess, sometimes it felt awkward. It was a monotonous daily grind but it was never boring!

I spoke to other mothers about their experiences and it seemed to me that there were three common themes of experience, and that is why I chose to write separate chapters on our experiences.

These three common themes are:

1. Friendship and support in the playground
2. Paranoia in the playground
3. Difficult situations between parents in the playground

Friendship and support in the playground

There is no doubt that the friendships developed in the playground are really special. They are supportive, helpful and caring. When starting Primary school with your first child, there are so many things to get to know and to worry about. After all, for many mums, it is the first time that their child will be taking their first steps to independence. It can feel a scary time or an exciting time and for many probably a bit of both. Friendships between mums help us navigate this transition and many friends that we make in those early years stay friends for life. But as we have seen some do not!

Paranoia in the playground

This is probably very common but difficult to admit! On days when I felt a bit low I could be standing next to a 'perfect' mummy and begin to feel 'not good enough'. And truth to tell I have also had days (probably less!) when I might feel a bit better than somebody else. The reference by Eric Berne goes into detail about the four life positions that we may find ourselves in (grounded, inferior, superior and hopeless). Grounded is the position to aim for, where we accept our differences and feel OK about ourselves and OK about others. This is not easy on an 'I'm running late with no make-up on' sort of day!

Difficult situations between parents in the playground

I could never have imagined how tricky things could get before I started on the school run. I had experience of nursing (one year), university (the most fun three years!) and working in organisations (many many years) before I embarked on motherhood. Of course there had been difficulties along the way but nothing prepared me for relationship difficulties in the playground. Separate from the children's difficulties (or so it seemed at first!) was the tricky relationships between parents - relationships between parents could be tortuous. In fact it was this area that made me think about the question 'what is going on here?'

Of course we should expect nothing less from Mother Tiger protecting her Cub. Mother and child are uniquely bonded and the relationships between parents are not independent. What upsets our children will upset us also. There is a parallel process that goes on between children in the playground and parents in the playground; happy children result in happy relationships between parents, but feuding children can often result in feuding parents. No matter how mature we are, we will hurt (and feel fury) for our children if they are unhappy and have been hurt by other children.

The school run offers us rich and sometimes challenging experiences. Was I glad when the school run was over – yes I was! Would I rather not have had the experience? Not at all! It has been both fascinating and challenging and from those experiences this book was born.

Endings at school and celebrations of a new beginning

As the school year comes to an end there is a sense of something very different happening for Year 6. The tension and excitement are tangible. All schools are likely to mark the end of Year 6 in some way that celebrates the ending of Primary school and paves the way for the next step to Secondary school.

In our Primary school there were five main areas that involved my children, these were:

1. End of year production
2. Musical concerts
3. End of year party at school (all children from Year 6)
4. Final Year 6 assembly
5. End of year party for class (organised by the mums)

End of year production

This was a great event and one much looked forward to by children and parents alike. The rehearsals and auditions began as early as the spring term and this was considered to be one of the most important and happy events for the school leavers. This event was very much enjoyed by parents and children alike. DVDs were made of both my children's productions and of course I bought both. Even now I find that my teenagers sometimes have a little look back at the DVDs or talk about the end of year production.

Musical concerts

If your child is involved in music in any way, there are likely to be concerts to mark the end of the school years and to celebrate all that has been achieved. Never let it be said that recorder is boring. I attended the most fantastic concert which actually reduced the head teacher to tears as well as the parents with a fantastic rendition of the Titanic theme tune. All credit to our recorder teacher who was, in fact, one of the musical mums giving her time voluntarily.

End of year party at school (all of Year 6)

It is likely that the school will put on a party for the whole of Year 6, maybe in the school hall. At our school this was organised by the school's parents committee which was made up of a group of volunteers. This was a great event and much loved by all children. The hall had been totally transformed for this event. The mums had worked really hard to give the children a great send off!

Final assembly for Year 6

This was the big tear-jerker for all. It was the true 'goodbye' on the last morning of the school term. Parents were invited and children talked about their fondest memories and also what they hoped to achieve in the future. Like a true ending it was about loss and goodbyes and a celebration of what had been achieved and what was yet to come. Not easy, but essential, to mark the ending in this way.

End of year party for the class (organised by the mums)

Sometime before the end of the year or just after the end of term a party is probably organised for the class. These parties are normally organised by two or three brilliant mums and my son's end of year party was a great event in a hall with a disco with lots of food and fun things to do. My daughter's class party was organised by several mums who provided the class with a James Bond themed party (including a James Bond car!). No stone was left unturned with regard to detail even down to the partners of the organisers dressing in formal black tie and the organisers dressed in long evening wear. Not all parties will be so elaborate – but the important thing is that the ending of Primary school is marked in a way that the form will enjoy and all groups will enjoy different activities. My thanks go to all the mums (the great organisers!) who gave up their time to provide our children with such a fitting send off.

All these ways of celebrating what has been achieved and marking the end of one phase of life are very important for moving on to the next stage - Secondary school.

Loss for parents

I just wanted to include this as a section as it is an important thing to recognise. While we are celebrating and looking forward to the next phase of our child's life we are also experiencing a loss. This is why our feelings can be so mixed when we get near to the end of the school year. So what exactly do we mean by loss? Loss can be experienced by many different events:

- Bereavement
- Divorce
- Retirement
- Redundancy
- Burglary
- Illness
- Ageing
- Children growing up

All these examples are events that involve change that is irreversible. There is no going back in situations such as these. If we were happy with the way things were, then we are likely to feel a sadness and loss of some kind.

It seems rather bad to be feeling a loss when our children are growing up and moving on, but it is a feeling felt by most parents, especially mothers. If it is your last child going to Secondary school or if you have only one child then these feelings may be more acute. So what are the things that make us feel sad? Everyone will be different but my list was as follows:

- End of one phase of life
- Child becoming more independent
- Not having the support of the Primary school
- The great unknown of Secondary school
- Not seeing my friends every day on the school run
- No more cosy classrooms that I can wander in and out of to see the teacher, collect lost property, look at the work on the walls

Everyone's list will be different, and maybe some parents will feel the loss more than others. Indeed a parent of many children may be really relieved that all their children are now in Secondary school.

However, if you do feel loss, it is easier to cope with if the ending is marked in a special way. This is why there are so many exciting events at the end of the school year for Year 6. It is both an ending and a new beginning for both child and parent.

Secondary school

This section is just a short section to look at our hopes and fears about Secondary school. In essence they are no different from our hopes and fears about starting Primary school. However there is one big difference. We have much less control over our children now as they become more independent. I worried so much when my son started Secondary school. He looked so small. I was sure he would be beaten up by some huge mean child on the way to school on his first morning. Luckily my fears were ungrounded and it wasn't long before he became one of the big ones. Just to share, these were some of my anxieties:

- Would he be bullied?
- Would he remember how to get to school?
- Would he remember how to get from class to class?
- What if he was hungry?
- What about the toilets, I'd heard rumours they locked them between lessons!
- Would he manage the lunch queue?
- Was his bag too heavy?
- Why wouldn't he wear a coat? (a recurring theme!)

It is good to know that actually my son navigated all of this (with or without a coat!). The only thing that really got on my nerves was that he would lose things all the time and now there was no going into school to look for them. However the main thing was he was coping and thriving and making friends and having some fun along the way. As he moved into adolescence I realised a whole new set of challenges were about to begin! But that is a topic for another book.

The life of work – groups and organisations

After Secondary school, and maybe further study or training, begins the life of work. I have put this section in because many of the things that our children are developing while they are playing in the playground are the things that are needed in our day-to-day interactions with people, and are needed in the world of work. Looking back at **Chapter 3, What our Children Learn in the Playground**, we can see that the following important topics were covered:

- Learning how to get on in a group
- Dealing with difficult situations and emotions
- Advanced social skills of empathy, negotiation and cooperation

Unless you work for yourself or have a very solitary job then it is likely that you will be working in a group. It may be a small group in a small firm or organisation or it may be a giant organisation like one of the big multinational organisations. If you work in a group you will need to get on with people and you will need to be able to navigate the challenges of being with people on a daily basis.

If you have a management position then the skills of negotiation and cooperation are key, and this cannot be done in a caring way without some empathy. How important to learn these skills. We begin to learn these skills - these building blocks of our working life - at home. They are fostered in preschool and then developed in Primary school. Negotiation and cooperation will not be developed without the acquisition of basic social skills (talking, listening and the art of conversation).

It is important to note here that our genetic differences will also have some (or a lot) of input into how well we develop these skills. Children who are on the Autistic Spectrum will find socialising difficult and empathy is a trait that these children do not develop well. However it is also important to note that many of our geniuses are on the Autistic Spectrum and will enjoy solitary or scientific jobs and are gifted individuals.

It is also important to realise that children who are having a very hard time at home (e.g. neglect or abuse) are unlikely to fulfil their potential either academically or socially. These children need our help and support.

The world of work is one that will touch most of us in our lives and getting ready for all the challenges is of paramount importance. And getting ready for these challenges begins in the playground! **The playground is a unique space for children to learn how to be with one another – it provides the opportunity for children to develop advanced social skills.** This is so important for our lives and future opportunities. Never let it be said that nothing important goes on in the exciting arena of the playground.

Top ten tips of advice

Giving advice needs to be done with caution and as a rule it is not something I do unless someone asks me what I would do in a situation. The big disadvantage of giving advice is that we may be wrong, and if someone follows our advice and it turn out to be a disaster, then it is likely that we will get the blame even if our initial motivation was to be helpful. The only person who can really decide what will work is you. You can listen to advice and suggestions and read information but at the end of the day the decision has to be yours. Never let someone push you into doing something you are not comfortable with.

Now I think I will change the title of this section to ....

My top ten tips for happy school run years

Parties

The first thing that I wish I had done differently was the number of children that we had invited to parties. As I mentioned in **Chapter 5, The School Run**, my son wanted to invite all the girls to his party in Year 2 which meant some of his friends had been left out. I had hoped that in Year 2 those that had not been invited would not notice, but I was wrong. Children do know who is invited and who isn't, and if I was starting again, I would make sure that I only invited a maximum of half the class, because if you invite more it does seem as if a select few have been left out. Usually it is a numbers thing but children do feel sad when they have not been invited especially if they are a friend. I still feel a bit awkward about what happened in my situation while I write this!

Be careful what you say in the playground

The playground is a hotbed of gossip and confidentiality is not a word that many take too seriously. My second tip is be careful what you say to people especially if it is about other people. Sad to say that even people who you believe to be friends at the start may not be by the end of Year 6. We can be left with thoughts like 'My goodness! What did I say to them?'

Beware of friendships of convenience

If you are a kindly sort of person you may find yourself doing more than your fair share of party runs and activity runs after school. The friendship will be sound until you may question the fairness or be unable to help as much. You may find the friendship ends as the friend in question moves on to find another helpful soul.

Expect some friendships to be of short duration

Remember in **Chapter 6, Friendship and Support in the Playground**, we talked about how parent and child are really one unit and how friendships can change if your child changes friendships. I believe that we must enjoy these friendships while they last as they enrich our lives but some will not endure a life time. Some mums would not worry about this at all, but I felt particularly sad when this happened as I was hoping to make new and long-lasting friendships. Some friendships are enduring and these are the ones to cherish. I have made some great friends during my time when my children were at Primary school and these are the friendships I hope will last a lifetime.

Do not expect everyone to behave well all the time

Maybe I was naive but I really thought we as parents would all behave as parents are expected to, and be good role models throughout. However I forgot that we are only human and that certain situations (and sometimes unconscious things) get in the way of this. I didn't know at the time about the unique dyadic relationship with our children. I had experienced the parallel process in counselling, but not anywhere else. I had not expected the depth of feelings of Mother Tiger when her Cub is hurt.

Do not expect yourself to be the perfect role model

I used to give myself such a hard time if I behaved in a way that I felt was 'not-OK'. These things could include shouting at the children to get them ready on time, being too stressed, crying, being late, getting cross when my son didn't want to do his spellings, cooking pizza from a packet too often, looking a bit of a mess, not ironing at all, having a sneaky cigarette when the children were in bed. I could go on and on – there were so many things that I did that were not perfect. I did my best. I guess that has to be good enough and now I realise that the pressure I put on myself to be the perfect mum was immense.

Expect to meet Mother Tiger in the jungle of the playground

It is inevitable that mothers will hurt for their children when things go wrong. The difficulty for us is there is little control over what our children do at school and we can't influence what they do or what they say to other children. We can't actually do anything about our child upsetting another child by accident or on purpose. It can be a jungle that needs to be navigated.

Forgive Mother Tiger.

Although she can make our life difficult and it can be painful standing in the playground with a mum who is upset with us, these mums are only hurting so much because they love their children and want them to be happy at school.

Expect to meet Mother Tiger in yourself

Don't expect to rise above all this 'nonsense' in the playground. If our child is hurt by another child or indeed a teacher we will find ourselves becoming the protector that our child needs.

Get involved with some school activities but be careful what those activities involve

There are many activities that you will be asked to help out with. Be careful to choose the ones you want to do. There are lots of good things to get involved with and some of the things that I really enjoyed were as follows: washing fruit for the infants one day a week, doing the collection and card for the end of year, helping out on the stalls on the day of the Summer Fete. Now that my children have moved on to Secondary school, I still go in one morning a week and read with Year 1 or Year 2 (such a dear age!). Other mums turned out to be brilliant party organisers and provided us with fabulous end of year parties. I rather admired these mums!

At the end of this chapter I have include a table of my top ten learning points. You will be able to draw up your own list as the years go by.

Celebrating motherhood

There is so much in the press these days about getting mothers back to work and getting children into childcare that I am beginning to feel that the government must be thinking that mothers are not necessarily the best people to look after their children! It is beginning to feel that working full time or part-time is the 'thing' to do. If we don't work we are being lazy and not contributing to society. Am I alone in thinking that the important point is that **motherhood and caring for our children is a vital contribution to society.** We are caring for the next generation who will be involved in the world of work, helping grow our economy and in fact will be looking after us in our old age! I believe that mothers should be supported to stay at home to look after their children if they want to and circumstances allow, and be recognised for this very important job!

I realise that for some mothers deciding whether to work or not is not an option, and I realise that some mothers will want to go back to work, but there are a lot or mums who work part-time or don't have paid work who are now beginning to feel that they 'ought' to be out there 'contributing'.

I really want to say that **we should be celebrating motherhood and recognising the fantastic (unpaid!) contribution we make to society.**

Last comments from the Author

What goes on in the playground is much more interesting than at first meets the eye! Children have an opportunity to develop their social skills and to learn what is right and what is wrong. They may even learn to say 'sorry'. They learn to develop the advanced social skills of empathy, negotiation and cooperation which are so important to our working lives in groups and in organisations. They will begin to experience competition with others. The playground is a unique space for children to learn how to be with one another – it provides the opportunity to develop advanced social skills.

As a mum I have made some very special friends from my years when my children were at Primary school. We have shared special times that I have not had with other friends in my life time. There were difficulties and upsets along the way and I made some mistakes that upset others. However it was a time of great joy and excitement. It is some of the very best years of our children's lives. If you are about to experience years of the school run you may feel daunted but you really will experience and learn so much.

My very final comment!

My very final comment is a plea to teachers! **Please don't keep persistently unfocussed and disruptive children in at their break-time as their punishment.** These children may have undiagnosed ADHD and can't help their behaviour. I know it seems as if they can behave sometimes, and maybe they can for short periods of effort, but keeping these children in at break time will just exacerbate the problems. Believe it or not these children are often really trying their best. ADHD can be a hidden disability (which does not have to involve hyperactivity) and affects 1-3% of children, maybe more. There is a reference at the end of this book which I would fully recommend to teachers and parents, and anyone else who is interested in the field of ADHD.

My top 10 tips for surviving the playground

1. Parties. Take care with number of invites

2. Be careful what you say to others in the playground

3. Beware of friendships of convenience

4. Expect some friendships to be of short duration

5. Don't expect everyone to behave well all the time

6. Don't expect to be the perfect role model

7. Expect to meet Mother Tiger

8. Forgive Mother Tiger

9. Expect to meet Mother Tiger in yourself

10. Get involved in some school activities (but choose wisely!)

Sue Jones

References and Further Reading

ADHD
Kewley,G.D. **ADHD: Recognition, Reality and Resolution**. Acer Press, 2001.

Attachment
Bowlby,J. **A Secure base.** Brunner-Routledge, 1988.
Pearce,C. **A Short Introduction to Attachment and Attachment Disorders.** Jessica Kingsley Publishers, 2009.

Autistic Spectrum
Attwood, T. **The Complete Guide to Asperger's Syndrome**. Jessica Kingsley Publishers, 2007.
Baron-Cohen,S and Bolton,P. **Autism – The Facts.** Oxford University Press, 2004.
Simone,R. **Aspergirls.** Jessica Kingsley Publishers, 2010.

Bullying
Alexander,J. **Bullies, Bigmouths and so-called Friends**. Hodder Children's Books, 2003.
Field,E.M. **Bully Blocking.** Jessica Kingsley Publishers, 2007.

Child Development
Berk,L.E. **Child Development.** Pearson, 2012.
Meggitt,C. **Child Development.** Pearson, 2012.

General
Gerhardt,S. **Why Love Matters.** Routledge, 2004.

Parties
Hammick,R. and Packer,C. **Children's Parties.** Ryland Peters and Small, 2006

Karmel,A. **Annabel Karmel's Complete Party Planner**. Ebury Press, 2000.

Parenting Support
Biddulf,S. **The Secret of Happy Children**. Harper Thorsons, 2012.
Biddulf,S. **Raising Boys**. Harper Thorsons, 2010.
Biddulf,S. **Steve Biddulf's Raising Girls.** Harper Thorsons, 2013.

Play
Bishop,J.C. and Curtis,M. **Play today in the Primary School Playground.** Open University Press, 2001
Brooking-Payne,K. **Games Children Play.** Hawthorne Press, 1998.
Murphy,A.P. **The Secret of Play**. Dorling Kindersley, 2008.

Transactional analysis
Stewart,I. and Joines,V. **TA Today**. Lifespace Publishing, 2012.

Useful Addresses

ADHD

The National Attention Deficit Disorder Information and Support Service (ADDISS)
Premier House
112, Station Road
Edgware
HA8 7BJ
020 8952 2800
www.addiss.co.uk

Learning Assessment and Neurocare Centre (LANC)
48-50, Springfield Road
Horsham
West Sussex
RH12 2PD
01403 240002
www.lanc.org.uk

Autistic Spectrum

The National Autistic Society
393, City Road
London
EC1V 1NG
www.autism.org.uk

The Burgess Autistic Trust
129, Southlands Road
Bromley
Kent
BR2 9QT
020 8464 2897
www.bromleyautistictrust.co.uk

Learning Assessment and Neurocare Centre (LANC)
48-50, Springfield Road
Horsham
West Sussex
RH12 2PD
01403 240002
www.lanc.org.uk

Bullying

The National Bullying Helpline
PO Box 1276
Swindon
SN25 4UX
0845 22 55 787
www.nationalbullyinghelpline.co.uk

Counselling

British Association for Counselling and Psychotherapy
BACP House
15, St John's Business Park
Lutterworth
LE17 4HB
01455 883300
www.bacp.co.uk

Primary School Children - Help and Support

Mumsnet
www.mumsnet.com

Netmums
www.netmums.com

Index

Sue Jones

www.ingramcontent.com/pod-product-compliance
Lightning Source LLC
Chambersburg PA
CBHW022133080426
42734CB00006B/339